YORK NOTES

FRANKENSTEIN

MARY SHELLEY

NOTES BY GLENNIS BYRON

Longman

York Press

The right of Glennis Byron to be identified as Author
of this Work has been asserted by her in accordance with the
Copyright, Designs and Patents Act 1988

YORK PRESS
322 Old Brompton Road, London SW5 9JH

PEARSON EDUCATION LIMITED
Edinburgh Gate, Harlow,
Essex CM20 2JE, United Kingdom
Associated companies, branches and representatives throughout the world

© Librairie du Liban *Publishers* 1998, 2004

First published 1998
This new and fully revised edition first published 2004
15 14 13 12 11

ISBN: 978-0-582-82301-3

Designed by Michelle Cannatella
Typeset by Land & Unwin (Data Sciences), Bugbrooke, Northamptonshire
Printed in China (EPC/11)

CONTENTS

PART FOUR
CRITICAL HISTORY

PART FIVE
BACKGROUND

PART ONE

INTRODUCTION

HOW TO STUDY A NOVEL

Studying a novel on your own requires self-discipline and a carefully thought-out work plan in order to be effective.

- You will need to read the novel more than once. Start by reading it quickly for pleasure, then read it slowly and thoroughly.

- On your second reading make detailed notes on the plot, characters and themes of the novel. Further readings will generate new ideas and help you to memorise the details of the story.

- Some of the characters will develop as the plot unfolds. How do your responses towards them change during the course of the novel?

- Think about how the novel is narrated. From whose point of view are events described?

- A novel may or may not present events chronologically: the time-scheme may be a key to its structure and organisation.

- What part do the settings play in the novel?

- Are words, images or incidents repeated so as to give the work a pattern? Do such patterns help you to understand the novel's themes?

- Identify what styles of language are used in the novel.

- What is the effect of the novel's ending? Is the action completed and closed, or left incomplete and open?

- Does the novel present a moral and just world?

- Cite exact sources for all quotations, whether from the text itself or from critical commentaries. Wherever possible find your own examples from the novel to back up your opinions.

- Always express your ideas in your own words.

These York Notes offer an introduction to *Frankenstein* and cannot substitute for close reading of the text and the study of secondary sources.

CHECK THE BOOK

Chris Baldick, *In Frankenstein's Shadow: Myth, Monstrosity and Nineteenth-century Writing*, 1990, offers a useful critical survey of the monster as a mythic image in nineteenth-century writing.

READING *FRANKENSTEIN*

CONTEXT

During the 1820s, even before Shelley was known to be the author of *Frankenstein*, there were several stage productions based on her story playing in London. The first was Richard Brinsley Peake's *Presumption; or The Fate of Frankenstein*, 1823, and the changes Peake made established the direction for most later film versions. He introduces an assistant, for example, the bumpkin Fritz, and the monster becomes mute. No longer an astute critic of society, the monster consequently develops into its traditional role as the visible embodiment of evil. For further information about the play, see **http://www.rc.umd.edu/editions/contemps/peake/**.

'And now, once again, I bid my hideous progeny go forth and prosper,' says Mary Shelley (p. 10), as she draws her 1831 Introduction to *Frankenstein* to a close.

Go forth and multiply she may well have said. *Frankenstein* has become one of our most enduring cultural myths. Reworked and rewritten in countless stage productions and films, the subject of wide-ranging critical interpretations, Shelley's 'hideous progeny' is challenged perhaps only by Bram Stoker's *Dracula* in the relentless grip it has held on our imaginations. Few first-time readers will come to the novel without a set of expectations fostered by images ranging from a badly stitched Boris Karloff to a sexually indeterminate Frank-n-furter in *The Rocky Horror Show*. Expecting to be impressed by a spectacular electrical sideshow when the monster is created, frightened by a grunting clumsy subhuman monster with neck bolts, touched by the creature's idyllic meeting with innocent little Maria among the daisies, or titillated by the heavings of a voluptuous Elizabeth, the reader may be surprised to find how little these images have to do with Shelley's novel. Given the popular tendency to call the monster Frankenstein, we may even be surprised to find that the monster is actually nameless and that Victor Frankenstein is his creator. Coming to the novel for the first time, our culturally produced expectations may well immediately conflict with the text we read.

To experience such conflict between expectations and experience in a first reading of *Frankenstein* is, in many ways, an appropriate introduction to the work. *Frankenstein* is a novel of conflict, and not only conflict in the obvious sense of the conflict between Victor and his monster or between the monster and society. Conflict begins even before we pick up the book. Should we choose the original 1818 edition or the revised 1831 edition? Shelley herself attempts to downplay differences by claiming the changes were relatively insignificant and mainly stylistic. Detailed comparisons have shown this not to be true. To cite just a few examples, in 1831

Victor is portrayed more sympathetically, the ideal nature of maternal love and the family is questioned, and Elizabeth, now far more passive and angelic, is no longer Victor's cousin, undercutting the more obvious incestuous overtones of the story (see **Note on the text**). The changes that were made seem to indicate yet another conflict: that between the more reactionary nineteen-year-old girl, Mary Godwin, who first produced the novel in 1818, and the more mature and conservative married woman, Mary Shelley, who revised the novel and wrote the introduction in 1831. While these notes will refer to the 1831 edition, the edition generally used for study, it is important to remember another version does exist.

Any attempt to find some fixed meaning in the novel only introduces further conflict. In giving life to his creature, Victor may be a Promethean rebel against God (see **Analogy and allusion**), an heroic quester after knowledge, refusing to accept limitations, seeking to benefit humanity. He may alternatively be driven only by an egotistical desire for personal glory. He may be attempting to usurp the role not of God but of woman, to eliminate sexual relations from the act of creation. If so, we need to consider what dark forces in his psyche drive him to reject normal sexuality. Why does he alienate himself from his family and friends and yet at the same time so repeatedly insist upon the pleasures of home and the satisfactions of domestic tranquillity?

In *Frankenstein* we are continually faced with irresolvable conflicts in interpretation. Initially, Shelley appears to set up a neat set of oppositions: good and evil, creator and creature, victimiser and victimised, monstrous and human, the isolated world of the intellectual and the communal world of domestic affections. A close reading of the text, however, shows the instability of all such oppositions, the difficulty of privileging one over the other in an attempt to find some 'message' in the novel, some fixed meaning. Victor, for example, is indeed the creator, but we must also remember that he is, certainly from the monster's perspective, also the destroyer: he destroys the female mate he is constructing and his life eventually becomes devoted to the destruction of his 'child'. So is he the **protagonist** of this novel or the **antagonist**? This seems to depend upon whose perspective is assumed. Is he an **anti-**

CHECK THE FILM

The 'classic' *Frankenstein* films are usually considered to be James Whale's 1931 *Frankenstein* and his 1935 *The Bride of Frankenstein*. These were, however, pre-dated by two American silent films, the Edison one-reel *Frankenstein*, 1910, and the first full-length version, *Life Without Soul*, 1915.

CONTEXT

Etymologically speaking, the 'monster' is something to be shown, something that serves to demonstrate (Latin, *monstrare*: to demonstrate) and to warn (Latin, *monere*: to warn). By providing a visible warning of the results of vice and folly, monsters promote virtuous behaviour.

CHECK THE NET

A useful site on film versions of *Frankenstein* is **http://members. aon.at/ frankenstein/**.

CONTEXT

In earlier Gothic fiction, evil is generally located primarily within an external source, in, for example, such horrifying figures as ghosts or demons, or in such institutions as the Roman Catholic Church, as demonised by Protestantism. With *Frankenstein*, the Gothic turns inwards, focusing more upon the evil within ourselves; haunted castles are replaced by haunted individuals, and a new Gothic figure, the double or doppelganger, emerges, the representation of an irreparable division within the human psyche.

hero? That does not seem quite appropriate either. Conversely, the creature may be a destructive 'monster', but he is also by nature a benevolent being, instinctively good. He becomes savage and violent only after he is rejected and shunned by all, only after he learns from his observation of humanity the meaning of anger and hatred and revenge. Is his violent behaviour monstrous then, or simply an indication of his growing humanity? He reveals, in many ways, a kindness and generosity of spirit rarely displayed by other characters in the novel. Who is the monster when he is stoned by the villagers? Who is the monster when he saves a drowning child and is shot by the child's father? It becomes more and more difficult to set the monstrous and the human in opposition. Roles become even more confused when we consider the repeated suggestion that the monster is Victor's **double**, 'my own vampire', as he says, 'my own spirit let loose from the grave, and forced to destroy all that was dear to me' (p. 77). It is quite feasible that all the savagery and violence are Victor's, repressed for many years, but now released, 'let loose' from his darker depths. Definition and categorisation are repeatedly called into question by the novel, and the figure of the creature itself becomes a sign for the confusion of categories and the difficulties of definition: it is living, but it is made of dead parts.

The pleasures to be gained from reading *Frankenstein* are not those we might expect from our experience of reworkings of the novel in twentieth-century films. Shelley hoped, as she says in her Introduction, to 'curdle the blood, and quicken the beatings of the heart' (p. 8). It is difficult, however, to do much curdling to a reader brought up on our Freddies and Jasons, difficult to elicit even one extra thump from the heart of a reader who can casually snack on popcorn while giant sharks snap at tasty limbs or Hannibal the Cannibal fixes dinner.

Nor are the pleasures those we associate with the satisfactions of finding **closure**, of encountering a neatly tied-up conclusion, clarifying for the reader a final meaning or moral message. While much popular horror of today is resoundingly conservative, determined to frighten us into conformity and setting the monster on all who stray from the straight and narrow, *Frankenstein* refuses to settle on any firm moral ground and constantly invites us to question comfortable assumptions. It encourages us to question accepted social and moral judgements, judgements about the nature of good and evil, the uses of scientific research, the value of such social institutions as the family, the Church, the legal system. It invites us to question assumptions about novels themselves: about the authority of author and text, about the nature of **genre**, the reliability of **narrative perspective**.

The novel that Shelley calls her 'hideous progeny' (p. 10) is, like the creature itself, stitched out of various miscellaneous parts that refuse to come together into a comfortable, acceptable whole. These notes will be concerned, therefore, not with offering one specific reading of *Frankenstein*, but with problematising *Frankenstein*, opening up a series of ways into the monstrous text that refuses us the satisfaction of easy judgements.

Frankenstein has become one of our most enduring cultural myths and has even provided us with a crucial **metaphor** for our modern world. While Shelley was obviously aware of the potentially negative consequences of developments in science and technology, in the twentieth century, we are simultaneously both more culturally reliant upon science and technology for our survival and even more aware of the dangers. After living through Hiroshima and Chernobyl and seeing chemicals destroy our wildlife and rip holes in the ozone layer, we recognise that it is the entire planet which is potentially under threat. Perhaps not surprisingly, therefore, we have imposed at least one clear, unambiguous moral on the novel. We have appropriated Shelley's *Frankenstein* to provide us with a metaphor for the potentially disastrous results of scientific aims pursued with a mindless disregard of potential human consequences. Most dictionaries now define a 'Frankenstein' as an agency that proves uncontrollable, a creation that slips from under the control of, and ultimately destroys, its creator. We have played our own variations on this modern idea of a 'Frankenstein,' with, for example, HAL in *2001, A Space Odyssey* and the replicants of *Bladerunner*. To reduce the meaning of Shelley's own tale to our twentieth-century dictionary definition, however, would be a mistake. It would be to disregard what is probably the most

CHECK THE NET

During the 1970s, Marvel published a short-lived series of comic books in which the monster was presented as a superhero. For a selection of images and a discussion, see **http://members. aon.at/ frankenstein/** and explore the comics link.

CHECK THE BOOK

Marilyn Butler's introduction to the Oxford World's Classics *Frankenstein. 1818 Text* provides an excellent discussion of Shelley's engagement with contemporary science.

CONTEXT

Mad scientists and artificial human beings were to become standard types of modern horror and science fiction and now often appear as robots, androids and cyborgs. The first fully developed robot in film is Maria from Fritz Lang's *Metropolis*,1927. Here the scientist Rotwang attempts to create his perfect submissive woman, but she rebels and provokes a worker's revolt before being finally burned at the stake.

disturbing alternative reading that *Frankenstein* provides: that the monster does *not* rebel, that the monster only compliantly acts out the repressed aggressions and desires of its supposedly civilised creator, and that if we are rushing towards disaster, then the disaster towards which we rush is of our own choosing.

PART TWO

THE TEXT

NOTE ON THE TEXT

The text used in compiling these Notes is the Oxford World's Classics *Frankenstein*, edited by M.K. Joseph, 1969. This is the 1831 text, published by Colburn & Bentley, which contained Shelley's final revisions. *Frankenstein* was first published by Lackington, Hughes, Harding, Mavor, and Jones in 1818. The changes made to the 1831 text were not just additions, or, as Shelley herself suggests in her Introduction, matters of style. Marilyn Butler's edition of the 1818 *Frankenstein*, Oxford, 1993, outlines many of the more substantive changes, including the addition of an inner life and more reflective nature for Victor, the softening of the characters, the rewriting of Victor's education, and the revision of family and blood-ties so that Elizabeth is no longer Victor's first cousin.

SYNOPSIS

Frankenstein is an account of the life of Victor Frankenstein as related by him to a British sailor, Robert Walton, by whom he has been found on the ice-floes of the Arctic ocean. Victor begins with an account of his family background in Geneva, his tranquil domestic life and the young orphan, Elizabeth, who becomes part of the household. His interest in science eventually takes him to the university at Ingolstadt, and his experiments lead him to the discovery of the secret of the life force. He constructs a human form out of dead tissue and brings the monster to life. Horrified by what he has created, he abandons his creation and experiences both a mental and physical breakdown. His friend Henry Clerval nurses him back to health. The monster seems to have disappeared. Victor receives a letter from his father telling him that his brother William has been murdered. He returns to Geneva and catches sight of the monster whom he assumes, rightly, to be the murderer. It is Justine, however, another member of the Frankenstein household, who is accused of the murder. Victor remains silent and she is

CONTEXT

The city of Geneva was admitted to the Swiss confederation in 1814. During the eighteenth and nineteenth centuries its reputation as an intellectual centre attracted many free thinkers, including Rousseau and Voltaire.

CONTEXT

Mary Shelley also pursues the idea of the restoration of life in a number of her short stories. 'Roger Dodsworth: The Re-animated Englishman', 1826, based on a popular hoax about an alleged revival, is a rather comic tale of a man found in a glacier and reanimated, and the incomplete 'Valerius; the Reanimated Roman' considers the rebirth of a body without its soul.

QUESTION

Does the creature bear responsibility for the suffering he causes, or should the blame ultimately be placed on Frankenstein?

executed. Tormented by guilt, Victor seeks solace in the Alps. Here he meets the monster who insists Victor should hear his side of the story.

The monster then provides a history of his life, starting with an account of his initial confusion at being abandoned in an alien world and the mistreatment he received from all he met. He hides in a hovel adjoining the cottage of the De Lacey family. Through observing and listening to them, he learns to speak and read. Benevolent by nature, the monster feels great affection for this family, whose story he relates. He reveals himself to them, believing in their compassion and generosity, but they drive him away in horror.

The monster, lonely and mistreated, soon becomes violent. He learns the identity of his creator and, out of a desire for revenge, murders William and incriminates Justine. At this point he promises Victor, whom he accuses of being irresponsible and cruel, that he will disappear and become benevolent once again if only Victor will create a female monster to be his companion.

Reluctantly, Victor agrees, but, finding the prospect loathsome, delays starting his task. His father suggests he should fulfil his mother's final wish and marry Elizabeth, but Victor instead leaves for Britain to begin work on the female companion. Clerval accompanies him as far as Perth in Scotland and then Victor proceeds to the Orkneys. The companion is nearly finished when he has second thoughts. At this moment he sees the monster at his window and tears the female to pieces. The monster, savage with rage, promises to be with him on his wedding night.

Victor goes out in a small boat to throw his scientific apparatus into the sea; his boat is blown to Ireland. Here, he is immediately arrested for the murder of Clerval, who has been found strangled on the shore. After spending some time in prison, Victor is found innocent and taken home by his father. He marries Elizabeth, and on their wedding night the monster murders her. Victor swears to devote himself to the pursuit and destruction of his monster and follows him to the Arctic Ocean where he is picked up by Walton.

Walton concludes the story by telling his sister of Victor's death. He finds the monster lamenting over the dead body, and the monster expresses his sorrow at what he has done and his determination to destroy himself by fire amidst the icy wastes of the North Pole. He springs from the cabin window and is gone.

DETAILED SUMMARIES

INTRODUCTION (1831)

- Mary Shelley describes the origin of her novel.
- At Byron's villa a ghost story competition is held.
- Mary Shelley has a dream.

Shelley provides an account of the origin of the novel. She describes both the general influences upon her writing and the specific events that led to the writing of *Frankenstein*: the competition to write a ghost story, the conversations with literary friends, and the dream that provided her with the idea of bringing dead matter to life.

COMMENTARY

The account has been shown to be unreliable in its particulars, immediately prompting us to ask how Shelley may be trying to influence the reader's response to the novel. We might similarly question the three **narrators** of *Frankenstein*. How do these narrators choose to present themselves and what effect are their **narratives** supposed to have on the listener or **narratee**? Are they reliable or unreliable narrators? (see **Narrative techniques**). Shelley's account of the novel's composition distances *Frankenstein* from the **Gothic tradition** and links it instead with what would later come to be known as Romanticism, in particular, with the Romantic interest in imagination and creativity (see **Literary background**). She links these concerns to current scientific ideas about the principle of life and the possible role of electricity in this

> **CONTEXT**
>
> During the summer of 1816, Percy and Mary Shelley, along with Byron and his physician friend, William Polidori, and Claire Clairmont, Mary's stepsister and Byron's lover, regularly gathered at Byron's villa beside Lake Leman. After amusing themselves reading from a collection of German Gothic tales one evening, Byron suggested a ghost story competition, and out of this competition Mary Shelley's *Frankenstein* emerged.

CONTEXT

Romanticism as a movement is generally considered to originate around 1789, the year of the French Revolution, and to end with the ascension of Victoria to the throne in 1837.

process (see **Historical background**). Shelley also provides one possible context for interpreting the novel: Frankenstein's creation is described as transgressing the laws of God and nature. Does the novel suggest Victor's main crime is to usurp the role of God as creator?

GLOSSARY

7	**Some volumes of ghost stories** J.B.B. Eyriès, *Fantasmagoriana, ou Recueil d'Histoires d'Apparitions de Spectres, Revenans, Fantômes, etc.; traduit de l'allemand, par un Amateur ,1812*
7	**Mazeppa** long poem by Lord Byron, published in 1819, describing the ordeal of a man tied to a demon horse which gallops over continents
7	**Tom of Coventry** the peeping Tom in the legend of Lady Godiva
8	**the tomb of the Capulets** scene of the tragic deaths in Shakespeare's *Romeo and Juliet*
8	**in Sanchean phrase** Sancho Panza is the squire in *Don Quixote* by Miguel de Cervantes (1547–1616); he is given to stating the obvious
8	**The Hindoos** according to Hindu mythology, the elephant which supports the world is Muhapudma, and the tortoise is Chukwa
8	**Columbus and his egg** Columbus, on the occasion when his discovery of America was belittled on the grounds that others had gone there since, challenged the company to balance an egg on one end. When all had failed, Columbus took an egg, cracked it, and let it stand on the broken end; as he demonstrated, it is easy to do anything once one is shown how
8	**Dr. Darwin** Erasmus Darwin (1731–1802), physician, poet, and evolutionist, grandfather of Charles. There is a brief discussion of spontaneous generation in his *Zoonomia* (1794–6)
8	**galvanism** the generation of electricity by chemical action, named after Luigi Galvani (1737–98), pioneer in the study of electricity

CONTEXT

The 1818 edition of *Frankenstein* was published anonymously and many readers and reviewers assumed it was the work of Percy Shelley because he had written the Preface. Percy Shelley is one of the major Romantic poets. His long poem *Alastor,*1816, is particularly interesting in the context of *Frankenstein*, and deals with many of the same issues, most notably, perhaps, the question of egocentricity.

PREFACE (1818)

- Percy Shelley, speaking as Mary, comments on the interest and intention of the novel.

- He speculates that the creation of artificial life may become feasible.

This Preface to the 1818 edition was written by Mary Shelley's husband, Percy. Speaking as though he were the author, Percy Shelley indicates that developments in science mean the creation of artificial life may become feasible. This fact distinguishes the novel from a 'mere tale of spectres or enchantment' (p. 13). *Frankenstein* offers the interest that lies in examining human reactions to what is strange and new, and the author has attempted to remain truthful to human nature in the manner of all great writers. Shelley suggests that the main intention of the novel is 'the exhibition of the amiableness of domestic affection, and the excellence of universal virtue' (p. 14). He concludes with a brief account of the story's genesis.

COMMENTARY

The degree of Percy Shelley's involvement in the writing of *Frankenstein* is much debated. He is alternately seen as a significant contributor or, as is much more likely, a minor collaborator. The reference to 'domestic affection' (p. 14) introduces one of the key themes of the novel (see **Themes**).

GLOSSARY

13	**The Iliad** Homer's epic poem concerning the Trojan war
13	**the tragic poetry of Greece** the three main Greek tragedians were Aeschylus (525–456BC), Sophocles (496–6BC), and Euripedes (480–6BC)
13	**Tempest** *The Tempest* ,1611/12, a play by Shakespeare dealing with strange experiences on a magical island
13	**Midsummer Night's Dream** *A Midsummer Night's Dream*, 1595/6, a play by Shakespeare dealing with magical events in a wood near Athens

CONTEXT

There was a growing cult of domesticity in the late eighteenth and early nineteenth century which involved an idealisation of family life: the home was seen as a refuge from the world and a site of value, a place of spiritual and emotional restoration, with the emphasis on the affections, the emotions and sympathetic engagement with others. The values of the cult of domesticity are to a great extent associated with the feminine, and the central figure is the devoted mother and wife, in charge of all moral and emotional matters.

LETTER 1

- Walton writes to his sister.
- His early life is described.

Robert Walton writes to Margaret Saville, his sister in England. He informs her of his safe arrival in St Petersburgh and expresses both his elation and his fears at the start of his expedition to the North Pole. Here he hopes to discover a tropical paradise. The letter allows for a recounting of the main events in Walton's life which have led him to this juncture.

COMMENTARY

Walton's **narrative** is the **frame** in which the other narratives are embedded (see **Narrative techniques**). Shelley begins in the **epistolary** style, presenting the story through a series of letters. In his character and his ambitions, Walton anticipates Victor Frankenstein. Like Victor, Walton rejects a life of domestic ease for a life of adventure and a quest for knowledge. In speaking of his quest to find the Pole, he alternates between revealing a desire for personal glory and a desire to benefit mankind in a manner which also anticipates Victor speaking of his quest to discover the secret of life. In the case of each man, it is useful to consider whether the altruistic motive is genuine or a cover for overwhelming ambition.

LETTER 2

- Walton writes of his progress to Archangel.
- He describes his crew.

Now in Archangel, Walton has hired a ship and begun to collect his crew. Here, he applauds the courage of his lieutenant, who like Walton himself is 'madly desirous of glory' (p.20), and of his ship's master, known for 'his gentleness and the mildness of his discipline'.

Walton again anticipates Frankenstein in the expression of his deep need for a sympathetic friend.

COMMENTARY

The idea of alienation, which plays a key role throughout the text, is introduced (see **Themes**). Victor's ambitions, like those of Walton, isolate him from his family and friends. Alienation is further emphasised by the **allusion** to Coleridge's *The Rime of the Ancient Mariner* (see **Analogy and allusion**). Walton's description of his ship's master suggests he is the embodiment of goodness, and many of *Frankenstein*'s minor characters appear as little more than representations of abstract qualities, a manner of representing character typical of the **Gothic** tradition. In the case of Victor and the monster, however, Shelley seems concerned with the kind of analysis of individual psychology we associate more with **realism**.

GLOSSARY	
19	*keeping* maintaining a proper relation between the representations of nearer and more distant objects in a picture, basically perspective, harmony
20	prize-money proceeds of the sale of enemy shipping and property captured at sea

LETTER 3

- Walton expresses confidence in his quest.
- He cannot bear to think of failure.

Except for the weather conditions and his distance from home, Walton has little to report here, but is confident in his ambition. 'What', he asks, 'can stop the determined heart and resolved will of man?' (p. 23)

COMMENTARY

One possible answer emerges in the next letter.

CONTEXT

Coleridge's *The Rime of the Ancient Mariner*, 1798, is a tale of sin and redemption. The mariner who tells the story was on a ship that was driven by storms to the Antarctic, 'the land of mist and snow'(p. 21) where it became locked in ice. The ship was visited by an albatross, a great sea bird, that seemed to befriend the men. They were glad to see the bird, and their luck improved: the ice broke up and a breeze from the south pushed them through the fog. Suddenly, in what seems an inexplicable act of perverse cruelty, the Mariner shot the bird, bringing a curse upon himself and his ship. In Part 4 of the poem, the mariner describes how he felt cursed after the death of all his companions when he is left 'Alone, alone, all all alone, / Alone on the wide wide sea'.

LETTER 4

- Walton catches a glimpse of the monster.
- The crew take Victor on board.
- Walton believes he has found a friend and confides his ambition.

This letter is written in three parts over a period of two weeks. In the first part, Walton and his crew grow despondent: the ship is trapped in the ice and they are unable to move. They are surprised to catch sight of a large being in a sledge, pulled by dogs. Soon after, the ice cracks, freeing the ship. The next morning, Walton finds his men talking to another man in a sledge, trying to persuade this frozen and emaciated traveller aboard. The stranger, Victor Frankenstein, agrees, but only after learning they are bound for the North Pole. Walton learns that he has been following the first figure they sighted, a figure the stranger refers to as the demon. His affection for his guest grows daily.

In the second part of this letter, Walton confides his ambitions to his new friend, who responds with dismay, arousing curiosity with the claim that he has been similarly driven by ambition and will tell his tale to dissuade Walton from continuing his quest.

The last part of the letter shows the stranger preparing to begin his tale. Walton resolves to record what he hears and to send the manuscript to his sister.

COMMENTARY

This letter emphasises the admiration and affection that Victor inspires in Walton, who sees great nobility, benevolence, and sweetness in this 'divine wanderer' (p.29). Do we later find these virtues in him? Part of the attraction seems to lie in his eloquence; the monster will be similarly eloquent (see **Language**). Our curiosity is aroused by the violence of Victor's outburst, the **melodramatic** nature of his language, and his reference to the demon.

QUESTION

Describe Robert Walton's scientific motivation and goals. How do they differ from those of Victor Frankenstein?

CHECK THE BOOK

For an interesting discussion of language in *Frankenstein*, see Peter Brook's '"Godlike Science/Unhallowed Arts": Language, Nature, and Monstrosity', in *The Endurance of Frankenstein*, eds. George Levine and U. C. Knoepflmacher, 1979.

GLOSSARY

24	**inequalities** irregularities of surface
24	**ground sea** a heavy sea with large waves

CHAPTER 1

- Victor gives an account of his parents and early upbringing.
- Elizabeth is introduced.

Victor begins with an account of his parents' courtship and marriage. His father, from Geneva and of distinguished ancestry, finds his bride-to-be weeping by the coffin of her father, his former friend. Impressed by Caroline's virtues and devotion, Alphonse becomes her protector and then her husband, retiring from public life. Victor is born in Naples, and enjoys a close and affectionate relationship with his parents, who guide him with a 'silken cord' (p.34). During one of Caroline's many charitable visits to the poor, she finds a beautiful child, Elizabeth Lavenza, whom the Frankensteins take into their home. Elizabeth becomes Victor's 'beautiful and adored companion' (p.35). A darker tone enters the narrative with his closing comment: 'my more than sister, since till death she was to be mine only' (p.36).

COMMENTARY

The **epistolary** style is now dropped. Victor's narrative is **embedded** within the **frame narrative** of Walton. A **dichotomy** is immediately suggested between the public sphere of work and action and the private sphere of the domestic affections. Caroline is represented as an ideal of femininity and Elizabeth as her apt pupil. The importance of physical beauty is stressed. Note also the religious **imagery** which colours all Victor's descriptions of Elizabeth; his later apparent rejection of mature sexuality may be linked to this early spiritualisation of women. While Victor paints a picture of an idyllic family life, he also begins to show the potentially stifling nature of the domestic world (see **Themes**).

CONTEXT

In the original version of 1818, Elizabeth is Victor Frankenstein's first cousin and some critics have suggested this hints at an incestuous relationship.

 QUESTION

How do the language and imagery used in association with Elizabeth suggest her character, and what does it tell us about the narrator's (Victor's) attitude towards women?

Chapter 1 continued

GLOSSARY

31	**syndics** chief magistrates of Geneva
32	**Reuss** river flowing through Lucerne
33	**exotic** a rare and tender plant
35	*schiavi ognor frementi* (Italian) 'slaves ever fretting' a reference to the current Italian unrest under Austrian rule
35	**chamois** type of antelope found in southern and central Europe

---

CHAPTER 2

- Clerval is introduced.
- Victor describes his early interest in science.

CONTEXT
Heinrich Cornelius Agrippa von Nettesheim (1486–1535) was a medieval scholar whose most famous work, *De Occulta Philosophia Libri Tres*,1531, explores magic, astrology, alchemy, medicine and more; it had a significant influence on the spread of the occult sciences. Agrippa is popularly best remembered for his disobedient apprentice who accidentally conjured up the devil.

Victor continues the account of his upbringing. Another son, Ernest, is born. His close friend, Henry Clerval, is introduced. Victor recalls the moment when he discovers a volume of Cornelius Agrippa, a German alchemist associated with the occult. Victor's father forbids him to waste his time with such 'sad trash' (p. 39), but Victor disobeys him and becomes fired with enthusiasm to find the elixir of life. During a thunderstorm he witnesses the power of nature and then learns about a new theory concerning electricity. While Victor and Clerval pursue their studies, Elizabeth reads poetry and contemplates the beauty of the world.

COMMENTARY

The division between male and female roles is emphasised, and the conflict between happy domestic life and intense personal ambition, the claims of the community and the individual, is now firmly established. Religious **imagery** is again used in descriptions of Elizabeth, whose concerns are limited to the family circle and who fills her time with 'trifling occupations' (p. 64) while Victor is filled with desire for knowledge. He establishes himself as a Promethean 'overreacher' by hungering after the secrets of heaven and earth. Electricity, the scientific equivalent of the fire stolen from the sun in the original myth, is established as the potential animating force to be used by this modern Prometheus (see **Analogy and allusion**).

 CHECK THE NET
Search for Maureen B. Roberts' '"Ethereal Chemicals": Alchemy and the Romantic Imagination', a 1997 essay in the on-line journal *Romanticism on the Net*.

GLOSSARY

37	**heroes of Roncesvalles** The subject of numerous poems, and in particular the *Chanson de Roland*. Roland and Oliver were knights who supposedly died during the defeat of the rearguard of Charlemagne's army at Roncesvalles, a valley in the western Pyrenees
37	**the chivalrous train** the Crusaders
37	**temperature** temperament
38	**Natural Philosophy** the physical sciences
38	**Thonon** on the southern French shore of Lake Geneva
	Paracelsus Theophrastus Bombastus von Hohenheim (1493–1541), was a Swiss physician and alchemist.
	Albertus Magnus was a German theologian (1193–1280) who studied the brain; he is associated with device of a brazen head that could answer questions
39	**Sir Isaac Newton** English scientist (1642–1727)
39	**tyros** beginners
	philosopher's stone was a hypothetical substance which the alchemists believed would convert base metal into gold.
	elixir of life was a supposed potion of the alchemist that would indefinitely prolong life.

CONTEXT

In 1746, Benjamin Franklin became the first to demonstrate that lightning is electricity. In 1751, he conducted his famous experiments with a kite – the following two people who tried to duplicate this experiment were killed by the lightning strike – and in 1752 he developed the lightning rod.

CHAPTER 3

- Caroline dies.
- Victor goes to university.

Victor is sent to the university of Ingolstadt in Bavaria. Before he leaves, his mother, having caught scarlet fever while nursing the afflicted Elizabeth, dies. Her deathbed wish is that Victor and

CHECK THE NET

Frankenstein: Penetrating the Secrets of Nature is a virtual exhibit that was developed as an online complement to an actual exhibit at the National Library of Medicine and explores the history, science, and hubris of mankind in the quest for immortality: **http://www.nlm.nih.gov/hmd/frankenstein/frankhome.html**.

CONTEXT

In the 1780s, the Italian professor of anatomy Luigi Galvani conducted experiments on animal tissue using a machine that produced electrical sparks. He wrongly concluded that animal tissue contained electricity in a fluid form, but rightly proved that muscles contracted in response to electrical stimulus, and his research led to many new discoveries about the operation of nerves and muscles.

Elizabeth should marry. Victor eventually leaves for Ingolstadt; while regretting that he must leave his family and friends, he is eager for new knowledge. He introduces himself to M. Krempe but is repelled by the physical appearance and manners of this professor of natural philosophy and makes little attempt to begin his studies. He eventually attends his first lecture and hears Waldman, whose charm, benevolence and inspirational words determine Victor to return to his old quest to discover the mysteries of creation.

COMMENTARY

Victor's reaction against the hot house of family life is suggested by his confession that he had often thought it hard to remain 'cooped up' (p. 45) in one place and had longed to enter the wider world. The importance of physical beauty is again stressed by his reactions to Krempe.

GLOSSARY	
45	'old familiar faces' from 'Old Familiar Faces', a poem by Charles Lamb
47	chimeras a chimera is a fabulous monster made of various parts of different animals; here, the term is used in its more general sense of idle or wild fancies

CHAPTER 4

- Victor discovers the secret of life.
- He relates how he constructed the monster.

Victor devotes himself to his studies and his progress is rapid. For two years he does not visit his family. Just when he is thinking of returning he discovers the secret of life. Victor has been studying anatomy and physiology. Examining not only the structure but also the decay of the body, he observes the corruption of death during days and nights in charnel houses and vaults. He becomes capable of 'bestowing animation upon lifeless matter' (p.52), and begins to create a frame of a man out of pieces of corpses. He describes the horrors of his midnight labours, the obsession which blinds him to everything, isolates him from all. His father writes to show his concern at a lack of communication. At this crucial point in his quest Victor is clearly ill, mentally and physically. He interrupts his narrative twice to address Walton, suggesting he regrets his efforts and his error was to reject domestic tranquillity. He offers himself as moral exemplar of the dangers of knowledge.

COMMENTARY

Victor isolates himself completely from family and friends, ignoring all attempts at communication. He aspires to usurp the roles of both God and women, to create a new species who would bless him as their creator. Victor's search for the principle of life is presented in scientific terms, making the rather fantastic quest more believable to the reader, and suggesting a material and secular answer to the question of life, once seen in purely spiritual, divine terms. However, we may be immediately suspicious of his ambition since his quest leads him from the start to death and corruption. His ambition may be heroic, but the horrific images of his 'secret toil' (p. 54) suggest his work is also sordid. The **imagery** also may be seen to suggest the process of labour and birth; the 'workshop of filthy creation' (p. 55) may be read as the womb, suggesting Victor's repugnance for normal sexuality. At the end of this chapter he behaves as though guilty of a terrible crime.

While Victor here seems to regret his search for the secret of life, more frequently, we feel it is not the efforts or the search he regrets but the result. He may here offer himself as an example of the dangers of overreaching, but this must be put beside his final refusal to deny the importance of the attempt and his belief that another may succeed. The question of whether Victor is right or wrong to pursue his quest is never really resolved.

> **CONTEXT**
>
> During the early 1800, there was an increasing demand for corpses to be used in training doctors in anatomy. The law ruled that only the bodies of recently executed criminals could be used, but there were not enough to meet demand; this consequently led to grave robbing, which many developed into a highly lucrative business.

 QUESTION

Is science, overall, presented as a negative or a positive endeavour in *Frankenstein*?

GLOSSARY

53	**like the Arabian** from the fourth voyage of Sinbad in *The Thousand and One Nights*

CHAPTER 5

- The monster comes to life.
- Victor breaks down but recovers.

CHECK THE FILM
One of the most notable film versions of the scene in which the monster is animated can be found in James Whale's *Bride of Frankenstein*, 1935. While many of the details are changed, you will probably find that it captures the spirit of the original text in some interesting ways.

Victor succeeds in infusing the frame he has constructed with life: the monster's dull yellow eye opens and it breathes. While we may expect Victor to be exultant, he is immediately filled with horror and disgust. The monster is ugly; the child he has produced is unnatural. He rushes away to his bedchamber, where he eventually falls asleep only to be tormented by a terrifying dream in which Elizabeth, as he kisses her, turns into the corpse of his dead mother. Awakening with a start, he sees, by the light of the moon, the monster looking at him with one hand stretched out; Victor again flees. The next day he momentarily forgets his horror when, to his delight, he encounters Henry Clerval, who has come to study in Ingolstadt. Clerval realises that he is ill and questions him. Victor breaks down completely. For several months he is nursed through his fever by Clerval. In the spring Victor begins to recover and receives a letter from Elizabeth.

COMMENTARY

QUESTION
What can we conclude about Frankenstein from a consideration of his personal relationships and his scientific project?

The atmosphere is appropriately dreary. While Shelley is not specific about how the animation of the monster is accomplished, Victor's early interest in electricity suggests this may be the 'spark of being' (p. 57). The description of the monster may suggest the appearance of a newborn child, but there is also the emphasis on the unnatural which reflects the manner in which it was created. Victor's horrific dream is highly **symbolic**, and can be interpreted in a variety of ways (see **Detailed commentaries: Text 1**). The pathos of the monster's situation is suggested by his outstretched hand. Victor immediately proves himself irresponsible by abandoning the child in horror.

The question of the monstrous is first problematised here by the way in which it is suggested to be little more than a discursive effect, the product of how the creature is represented by others.

Frankenstein, an unreliable narrator at best, repeatedly misreads such things as the creature's gesture towards him at the moment of animation, and the creature's words regarding his wedding night; later, he even assumes the food and clothing left for him as he pursues the creature must come from some guardian angel. It is, of course, left by the creature himself, but Frankenstein reveals a mind determined to impose coherence in accordance with his own understanding of himself as a victim and his creature as an monstrous force to be eliminated. His language, as much as any act of the creature, functions to produce monstrosity.

As Victor wanders the streets, the quotation from Coleridge's *The Rime of the Ancient Mariner* suggests he is now full of fear and guilt, haunted by a nameless horror (see **Analogy and allusion**). He has a complete mental and physical breakdown, and when he recovers, descriptions of spring, with the young buds on the trees, suggest a new start; he dismisses thoughts of the monster from his mind.

 CHECK THE NET
Search for a discussion of some parallels between *Frankenstein* and *The Rime of the Ancient Mariner*.

GLOSSARY

58	**Dante** Italian poet (1265–1321), author of *The Divine Comedy*, divided into books focusing on Hell, Purgatory, and Paradise
60	**Vicar of Wakefield** novel by Oliver Goldsmith (1730–74); the 'schoolmaster' is the Principal of the University of Louvain

---

CHAPTER 6

- A letter from Elizabeth about the family arrives.
- Victor convalesces.

The first part of this chapter transcribes Elizabeth's letter. She offers her sympathy and provides news of the family. Much of the letter is devoted to the story of the gentle Justine Moritz who, after years of being mistreated by her mother, has become a servant in the household, but is regarded as one of the family.

CHECK THE NET
The Romantic circles Praxis series, an online journal, has an issue on *Romanticism and Ecology*, edited by James McKusick, that offers a selection of useful articles dealing with Romantics and nature: **http:// www.rc.umd.edu/ praxis/ecology/**.

The second half of the chapter details Victor's convalescence. He can no longer bear to think of his scientific studies. The two friends begin a tour of the region in May and Victor is revived by the company and the charms of nature.

COMMENTARY

Elizabeth's description of the treatment of servants provides Shelley with the opportunity for commenting upon social injustice. Justine's background, with its suggestions of incestuous impulses in her father's fondness and clear evidence of abuse in her mother's treatment of her, offers a new perspective on family life and the domestic affections.

The chapter concludes with more images of spring and an emphasis on the beauties of nature and the delights of community. Although Victor seems to be lulled into a false sense of security, these idyllic descriptions only increase tension for the reader who, unlike Victor, has not forgotten the monster.

GLOSSARY

65	**Ariosto** Angelica is the princess of Cathay in *Orlando Furioso* by Ludovico Ariosto (1474–1533)
69	**manly and heroical poetry of Greece and Rome** such as the epics of Homer (*The Iliad* and *The Odyssey*) and Virgil (*The Aeneid*)

CHAPTER 7

- William is murdered.
- Victor sees the monster on his journey home.

Victor receives a letter from his father, informing him of the death of his young brother William. The child had been found with the print of the murderer's finger on his neck. Victor begins the journey home and on the way he visits the spot where William had been murdered.

He is caught in a storm and glimpses, in a flash of lightning, the figure of the monster. Convinced that his creation is the murderer, he wanders throughout the night reflecting upon the evil to which he gave birth. In the morning he returns to his family to discover that Justine has been accused of the crime. Victor meets Elizabeth again; she hopes that he will be able to prove Justine's innocence.

COMMENTARY

In going to the place where William was strangled, Victor appears like a guilt-ridden murderer revisiting the scene of his crime. This, combined with his description of the monster as 'my own vampire, my own spirit let loose from the grave' (p. 77), introduces the idea of the **double**. The monster may be seen as an externalisation of a repressed part of Victor's psyche (see **Themes**).

GLOSSARY	
71	**Plainpalais** a popular promenade on the outskirts of Geneva
74	**cabriolet** a light two-wheeled, one-horse carriage
74	**Lausanne** resort on the northern shore of Lake Geneva
74	**'the palaces of nature'** from Byron's *Childe Harold's Pilgrimage*
74	**Jura** mountains along the Franco-Swiss border
77	**Salêve** Mount Salêve, south and west of Geneva

CHAPTER 8

- Justine is tried for murder.
- She is found guilty and executed.

Victor reports on the trial of Justine. The evidence against her appears strong. Elizabeth speaks in her defence, but while the court is moved by her benevolence and loyalty, it is not moved in favour of Justine, who now simply appears all the more ungrateful to her

CONTEXT

Another Gothic story that focuses on the idea of the double or doppelganger (from the German, 'double goer') is Robert Louis Stevenson's *The Strange Case of Dr Jekyll and Mr Hyde*, 1886, where Hyde, an atavistic figure of violence and excess, functions as the doppelganger for Jekyll, whose unacceptable desires he acts out.

 QUESTION

To what extent can Elizabeth's attitude towards Justine and her sufferings be said to reproduce the egocentricity revealed by Victor Frankenstein?

CONTEXT

In her criticism of society, Shelley frequently echoes the ideas of her father, William Godwin, one of the most influential political radicals of his time. Godwin was the author of the political treatise, the *Enquiry Concerning Political Justice*, 1793. He also wrote two Gothic novels: *The Adventure of Caleb Williams*, 1794, with its brooding atmosphere of religious terror and its exploration of guilt and persecution, and *St Leon: A Tale of the Sixteenth Century*, 1799, with its Promethean overreacher who receives the gift of the philosopher's stone and eternal life from a Wandering Jew figure.

kind employers. Victor, perceiving that Justine will be found guilty, rushes out of the court. In the morning, Justine is condemned, and Victor is told she has confessed. She asks to see Elizabeth who, along with Victor, goes to the prison; they discover that the confession was forced. Nevertheless all appeals are in vain and Justine dies on the scaffold.

COMMENTARY

Shelley uses the story of Justine to criticise social institutions, drawing attention to the corruption of both the Church and the legal system. The failure of Elizabeth's speech to help Justine shows her impotence when forced to deal with the outer world (see **Themes**, on **The critique of society**, and **Characterisation**, on **Elizabeth**).

Shelley now suggests that true horror lies within, in the mental agonies and torments we frequently inflict upon ourselves. Victor sees himself as the true murderer: 'I bore a hell within me' (p. 139), he says, echoing Satan in Milton's *Paradise Lost*, a work which will now play a significant role in the story (see **Analogy and allusion**). Victor's egotism and self-absorption are also revealed, however, when he attempts to describe his anguish, claiming that the 'tortures of the accused did not equal mine' (p. 85). Such claims as 'I cannot pretend to describe what I then felt' (p. 85) indicate the inadequacy of language to describe inner experience (see **Language**).

GLOSSARY

85   the ballots small coloured balls used for secret voting

CHAPTER 9

- Victor isolates himself from his family.
- His mental anguish grows.

Full of remorse and guilt, Victor again begins to shun his family and friends; he is tempted by suicide but fears to leave those he loves to the 'malice of the fiend' (p. 91). He attempts to forget his sorrows by immersing himself in the magnificence of nature and sets off for the valley of Chamo[u]nix.

COMMENTARY

Elizabeth's comment on the death of Justine, 'men appear to me as monsters thirsting for each other's blood' (p. 92), provides more social criticism, blurs the boundaries between the monstrous and the human, and encourages us to consider how we define 'monster' (see **Themes**).

Victor's language in this chapter repeatedly suggests the idea of the **double** 'I wandered like an evil spirit,' he says, 'for I had committed deeds of mischief beyond description horrible' (p. 90). Similarly, he speaks of the fiend that lurks in his heart. Again he shuns the company of family and friends. The descriptions of the cold high mountains and immense glaciers that conclude the chapter further emphasise his alienation from human affections, while the thunder and lightning signal the reappearance of the monster.

> **GLOSSARY**
>
> | 94 | a type of me a prefiguration; in typology, the scapegoat, for example, is a type of Christ; more generally, an image or figure |
> | 95 | aiguilles literally, needles, a reference to the sharp peaks of Mont Blanc |

CHAPTER 10

- Victor is in the mountains.
- The monster appears and they argue.

Victor gains some comfort from the **sublime** scenes around him. He resolves to ascend the summit of Montanvert. Gazing upon Mont

---

CONTEXT

Percy Shelley wrote a poem called 'Mont Blanc: Lines Written in the Vale of Chamouni'; an e-text can be found at **http://www.victorianweb.org/previctorian/shelley/montblanc.text.html**. As this poem suggests, for the English Romantic poets the natural world is pervaded by revolutionary energies, with both life-giving potential and the terrible power of destruction.

CHECK THE NET

For a brief summary of the Romantic position on Satan, see **http://www.wwnorton.com/nrl/english/NAEL/NAEL72/** and explore the Romantic Period link.

Blanc, he is filled with joy. At that moment, he sees the figure of a man approaching him with superhuman speed, bounding over the icy crevices. It is the monster. Victor, full of rage and horror, rejects him. The demon, as Victor now often calls him, complains of being abandoned. Instead of being like Adam in Eden, he is, he claims, more like a fallen angel, unreasonably driven from heaven. Only 'misery made me a fiend' (p. 100), he tells Victor. 'Make me happy and I shall again be virtuous.' (p. 100) This crucial speech from the monster convinces Victor that he should listen, and they proceed to a hut where the monster begins to tell his story.

COMMENTARY

While Victor describes him as 'devil', 'fiend', and 'vile insect' (p. 99), the monster surprises us by speaking with eloquence and dignity; his language assumes a biblical solemnity. It is Victor who rages with savage passion. The monster's situation evokes our sympathy, and he underlines Victor's crime in refusing to nurture his creation. Further references to *Paradise Lost* complicate the **analogies** between Victor as God the creator and the monster as Adam the created (see **Analogy and allusion**). The contrast between what is heard and what is seen is emphasised as Victor is persuaded by the eloquence of the ugly creature to listen to his story (see **Detailed commentaries: Text 2**).

CONTEXT

When thinking about the question of narrators and narratees in *Frankenstein*, remember that Margaret Saville is the only character who, like us, *reads* the story; the other characters *hear* versions of the story – Victor hears the monster, and Walton hears Victor. This may come to seem increasingly significant as Shelley draws our attention to the power of the speaking voice to persuade and seduce.

GLOSSARY		
96	presence-chamber	room in which the sovereign receives guests
97	Montanvert	viewpoint above Chamonix
97	concussion of air	disturbance of air
98	'We rest ... mutability!'	from Percy Shelley's 'Mutability', 1816
99	maw	mouth

CHAPTER 11

- The monster describes his early life.
- The De Laceys are introduced.

The monster begins the first of six chapters relating his story. He opens with vague memories of his first consciousness and the discovery of sensations. He seeks refuge in a forest, and discovers the use of fire, but remains in dire need of food and shelter. The humans he encounters react with fear, and he is driven out of a village. He finds a low hovel, adjoined to a cottage belonging to the De Lacey family, and makes this his home.

COMMENTARY

In this innermost **embedded narrative**, Walton is writing down the story told first by the monster to Victor and now by Victor to him. The monster appears like a natural man or **noble savage**, essentially benevolent, and we begin to see how this innocent has his psyche formed by his contact with the world. He is drawn to civilisation, but the civilised world rejects him on the basis of his alien appearance. From watching the De Lacey family, he learns more about emotion, about love.

 QUESTION

What is the function of the De Lacey family in *Frankenstein*. Is this, perhaps, where the text locates an alternative domestic ideal, or is the idealisation of the family unit qualified even here?

GLOSSARY

106	**Pandæmonium** the city built in Hell by the Fallen Angels in *Paradise Lost*

CHAPTER 12

- The monster learns language from the De Laceys.
- He is shocked to see his own reflection in a pool.

The monster begins to learn from watching the De Lacey family. Observing their poverty, he begins to help them as he can, cutting

QUESTION

Compare the educations of Victor Frankenstein and the monster. How do their differing educations influence their later actions?

wood during the night. He starts also to learn the rudiments of language from listening to their conversations. Admiring their beauty, he is shocked to view himself in a pool, and filled with shame and despondency at what he views as his deformities. Nevertheless, their gentle and affectionate natures lead him to imagine that they might receive him with kindness should he be able to win their good opinion. He consequently applies himself with new determination to the acquisition of language, and hope gives him happiness.

COMMENTARY

The De Laceys provide another example of idyllic family life, and the monster longs to be a part of this. His discovery of his ugliness in a pool is a **parody** of Eve's discovery of her beauty in the pool of Eden in Book IV of *Paradise Lost*. He begins to believe in the power of language to overcome the disability of his physical appearance.

GLOSSARY	
111	viands foodstuffs
115	the ass and the lap-dog Jean de La Fontaine (1621–95), *Fables* 4.5. The ass sees the lap-dog petted for fawning on its master, tries the same trick and is beaten

CHAPTER 13

CONTEXT

Constantin François de Chasseboeuf, Comte de Volney (1757–1820) was a moderate revolutionary and deist; his *Ruins of Empire[s]* was published in 1791.

- Safie arrives.
- The monster learns more about human nature.

A beautiful Arabian woman arrives with whom Felix De Lacey is clearly in love. The woman, Safie, is taught English by the family and the monster profits by the lessons. Felix tutors her with the aid of Volney's *Ruins of Empire[s]*, which provides the monster with the rudiments of the history, politics, and religion of various nations. He wonders at the dual nature of man, 'at once so powerful, so virtuous and magnificent, yet so vicious and base' (p. 119). The most important thing he learns is the cruelty of man towards what is alien and different, and with this comes understanding that he, with no family, friends, position, cursed with a deformed and loathsome exterior, is the ultimate alien: 'what was I?…I saw and heard of none like me,' he asks, and can answer only with groans (p. 120).

COMMENTARY

The monster's education provides Shelley with another opportunity for a critique of society and human injustice; once again, the boundaries between the monstrous and the human seem blurred (see **Themes**).

CHAPTER 14

- We learn the history of the De Lacey family.
- The story of Safie and her father is told.

QUESTION

The story of Safie is one of numerous sub-plots in the text. What contribution does it make to the novel and what would be different if it were omitted?

The history of the De Lacey family is gradually pieced together by the monster. They are French and of good family. Their story is closely tied in with the story of Safie and her father. He, a Turkish merchant living in Paris, had been condemned to death for a relatively minor crime. Felix, indignant at the injustice, planned his escape, meanwhile falling in love with the daughter Safie, who had been taught independence by her Christian mother. The plan succeeded, Felix's plot was discovered, and his father and Agatha were thrown in prison. On their release, the financially ruined De Laceys take asylum in Germany, and Safie eventually manages to make her way to their new home.

COMMENTARY

The rather bizarre and improbable adventures related here both provide Shelley with another opportunity to comment upon the corruption of society and also establish that the De Laceys and

CONTEXT

Mary Shelley's mother, Mary Wollstonecraft (1759–1797) is best known as the author of *A Vindication of the Rights of Woman* (1792), in which she called for the creation of equal rights and opportunities for women. A useful summary of her life and works can be found at http://www. philosophypages. com/ph/woll.html.

CHECK THE BOOK

A useful essay which places the education of the monster in context is Alan Richardson, 'From *Emile* to *Frankenstein*: The Education of Monsters' in his *Literature, Education and Romanticism; Reading as Social Practice, 1780–1832*, Cambridge University Press, 1994.

Safie, like the monster, are aliens and exiles. There is also a critique of the treatment of women. The portrayal of Safie, who combines both masculine and feminine qualities, suggests Shelley does not consider the passivity and helplessness of Elizabeth as either positive or inevitable (see **Characterisation**).

GLOSSARY

122	**Constantinople**	now called Istanbul
124	**haram**	women's quarters in a Muslim household
124	**Leghorn**	Livorno, Italy
125	**noisome**	foul-smelling
125	**asylum**	here used to suggest refuge
126	**confidential servant**	trusted servant

CHAPTER 15

- The monster discovers three books.
- He learns the identity of his creator.
- He approaches the De Laceys and is repulsed.

The monster relates a key incident in his narrative: the discovery in the woods of three books: *Paradise Lost*, a volume of Plutarch's *Lives*, and *The Sorrows of Wert[h]er*. He also discovers, in the clothing he took from the laboratory, Victor's journal from the months preceding the creation. From this he learns the repulsion felt by his creator and curses Victor for abandoning him. The monster eventually decides to approach the blind father when he is alone, since the horror of his appearance will not interfere with the man's judgement. All goes well until Felix, Safie, and Agatha enter. Felix flings him from the old man and beats him violently with a stick until the monster leaves the cottage and returns to his hovel.

COMMENTARY

The reading of the three books plays a crucial role in the development of his character and explains why the monster speaks as he does. *The Sorrows of Wert[h]er* expands his sensibilities, and he applies the story to his own feelings and condition, intensifying his sense of alienation. While from Werther he learns 'despondency and gloom' (p. 128), from Plutarch he learns 'high thoughts' (p. 128); he is raised beyond the misery of his own condition by the stories of heroes past. His admiration for virtue increases. *Paradise Lost*, however, is the most important of the three volumes. The monster sees his links with Adam, the first man, but sees also how they differ. Adam was happy and prosperous, cared for by his creator. He is wretched and alone, and thrown out of his Eden with no Eve to comfort him. Satan frequently seems a fitter comparison: when the monster observes the happiness of others he is eaten up with envy.

When the De Laceys reject the monster in horror, Shelley suggests again how appearance is privileged in this society. Even these paragons of virtue cannot deal with what is alien and different, and the idyllic nature of their domestic life is sustained only by the absolute exclusion of anything that may threaten it from outside.

GLOSSARY

128	**'The path of my departure was free'** Percy Bysshe Shelley, 'Mutability' 1.14 'The path of its departure still is free'
129	**Numa** Numa Pompilius (fl c.700BC), traditionally considered second of the seven kings of ancient Rome
129	**Solon** Greek statesman and legislator (c.630–c.560BC)
129	**Lycurgus** traditionally considered the lawgiver who founded the institutions of Sparta
129	**Romulus** legendary founder of Rome
129	**Theseus** legendary Greek hero
131	**Adam's supplication** *Paradise Lost*: either 8.379–97 or 10.743–45, which Shelley used as the epigraph to *Frankenstein*

CHAPTER 16

- We learn of the monster's rage.
- William's murder is explained.
- The monster demands a mate.

QUESTION

Contrasting markedly with his creator's evident reluctance to settle his 'union' with Elizabeth, the creature's desire for companionship is one of his most human qualities. Do you agree?

His hopes destroyed, the monster is full of anguish and rage at this treatment. The De Laceys depart, and the monster burns down their cottage. He then starts out for Geneva, determined to seek help from Victor Frankenstein. During his journey he is wounded by a man with a gun when he saves a young girl from drowning and this further inflames his feelings of hatred for mankind. Arriving on the outskirts of Geneva one evening, he falls asleep in the fields, only to be woken by the appearance of a beautiful little boy. Reasoning that the child will still be unprejudiced, he seizes him, planning to make him a companion and friend. The child, who turns out to be William, resists and reveals himself to be a Frankenstein. The monster, desiring revenge, strangles him. He sees the miniature of Caroline on the child's breast and the woman's beauty 'softened and attracted' (p. 143) him, but his rage returns. Coming across Justine sleeping in a barn, he plants the miniature on her. This chapter, and the monster's narrative, ends with this demand: Frankenstein must create a female companion to be his mate (see **Detailed commentaries: Text 3**).

CHECK THE FILM

The scene in which the artificial being asks for a female mate has been reworked in numerous other stories. In Episode 138 of *Star Trek*, 'Ship in a Bottle', for example, the holographic creature asks for a mate but his request is denied.

COMMENTARY

The monster experiences feelings of revenge and hatred for the first time, indicating how his character is being influenced by his interaction with human society. Comparing himself to the arch-fiend with a hell within him, he becomes more like Satan than Adam. William's reaction to his appearance suggests how quickly children are educated in society's prejudices.

GLOSSARY

136	**toils** nets
136	**a hell within me** *Paradise Lost* 9.467 'the hot hell that always in him burns'
139	**with the world before me** an echo of the end of *Paradise Lost* where Adam and Eve leave Eden

CHAPTER 17

- Victor eventually agrees to make a female.
- He returns to Geneva.

Victor initially refuses his request. The monster attempts to persuade him with reason, arguing that a female companion would return him to his previous benevolent and harmless state. After long reflection, Victor is eventually persuaded, considering that this would do justice to both his fellow beings and to his creation. The monster swears that he will disappear into exile with his mate and then suddenly leaves. Victor immediately returns to Geneva, resolved to save his remaining family and friends by complying with the monster's request.

COMMENTARY

The monster's eloquence persuades Victor, although the sight of the 'filthy mass that moved and talked' (p. 147) fills him with hatred. Language here appears to have the power the monster hoped it would have when he approached the De Lacey family. Victor now becomes even more alienated from his family.

GLOSSARY

149	**siroc** sirocco, a hot oppressive wind blowing from North Africa over the Mediterranean

---

CHAPTER 18

- Marriage with Elizabeth is suggested.
- Victor leaves for Britain with Clerval.

Victor is reluctant to begin his task and spends many melancholy weeks in Geneva. After he returns from one of his solitary rambles,

CHECK THE NET

Shelley Jackson's hypertext, Patchwork Girl, considered one of the most successful efforts in this medium, takes as its premise the idea that the female companion that Frankenstein begins creating but then destroys was secretly finished by Mary Shelley herself. To find out more about this hypertext, go to **http://www. eastgate.com/ catalog/ PatchworkGirl. html**.

CONTEXT

Mary Shelley wrote travelogues as well as fiction. *History of a Six Weeks' Tour*, 1817, was written with Percy Shelley and based on their elopement to the Continent in 1814. *Rambles in Germany and Italy*, 1844, concerns her recollections of later travelling with her son and his friends in search of improved health.

his father brings up the subject of his expected marriage to Elizabeth. Victor is filled with 'horror and dismay' at the thought of 'an immediate union' (p. 151). He decides he must create the monster's companion before his marriage takes place and leaves for England, being reluctant to carry out the work in his father's house. It is arranged that Clerval should initially join him on his travels. The chapter concludes with a description of their journey through Germany and Holland, their departure from Rotterdam and their arrival in London.

COMMENTARY

There seems to be more to Victor's reaction to the prospect of marriage with Elizabeth than meets the eye: his 'horror and dismay' (p. 151) are somewhat excessive. Fearing the monster he also fears his own sexuality. This may be confirmed by his tendency to refer repeatedly to a 'union' (e.g. p. 151) rather than a marriage. Victor's **panegyric** on his friend is a clear indication that Clerval will be the next victim.

GLOSSARY

149	**disquisition** research
149	**philosopher** scientist
151	**competent fortune** sufficient money on which to live comfortably
154	**bourne** destination, goal
156	**'the very poetry of nature'** ascribed by Shelley in the 1818 edition to Leigh Hunt's *The Story of Rimini*, a narrative poem on the love affair of Paolo and Francesca
157	**Spanish armada** fleet sent by Philip II of Spain against England in 1588

CHAPTER 19

- Victor leaves for the Orkneys.
- He begins to create the female.

Victor and Henry spend some time in London and then set off for Scotland. Much of this chapter is devoted to a description of the countryside. In Perth, Victor tells Clerval that he wishes to tour Scotland alone, and he travels to one of the remotest Orkney islands to begin his new creation. He hires a hut and is soon well advanced in the labour which to him becomes each day 'more horrible and irksome' (p. 164). He is filled with vague forebodings of evil.

COMMENTARY

This chapter is reminiscent of the travelogues which became so popular in the nineteenth century. Victor once again alienates himself from others in order to carry out his task. The enthusiasm he had felt in creating his first creature is now replaced by horror for the 'filthy process' (p. 164).

> **CONTEXT**
>
> The Orkney Islands lie off the northern tip of Scotland where the North Sea and the Atlantic Ocean meet. Orkney consists of around 70 islands; today only 16 of these are inhabited.

GLOSSARY

159	**Charles I** Charles I (1600–49) was executed after his defeat in the Civil War
159	**Falkland** Lucius Carey, Viscount Falkland (1610–43), Secretary of State under Charles I
159	**Goring** George, Baron Goring (1608–57), royalist general
160	**Isis** name given to the River Thames at Oxford
160	**verdure** fresh greenness
160	*ennui* weariness or languor brought about by boredom
160	**Hampden** John Hampden (1594–1643), Parliamentarian, mortally wounded at Chalgrove Field
161	**wondrous cave** probably High Tor Grotto near Matlock

CHAPTER 20

- Victor has second thoughts.
- The monster appears.
- Victor tears the female apart.
- The monster leaves with a threat.
- Victor is washed ashore in Ireland and arrested for murder.

QUESTION

Examine Frankenstein's considerations in this chapter, and his reasons for choosing not to create a mate for the creature, and compare them with his reasons for creating the creature in the first place. Has Frankenstein learned anything?

QUESTION

The scene which ends with the monster's chilling threat, 'I shall be with you on your wedding night', is one of three connected moments when the monster is seen at the window, in the moonlight, with a 'ghastly grin' on his face. What are the other two scenes, and why do you think the connection between these scenes is made so emphatically?

Victor, increasingly sickened by his task, begins to consider further the potentially disastrous effects of creating a mate for the monster. The monster appears at the window, and, reading malignancy in his ghastly grin, Victor tears apart the new creation before his eyes. The monster howls in despair and leaves, but soon returns and utters the chilling words: 'I shall be with you on your wedding-night' (p. 168). Victor receives a letter from Clerval and agrees to join him for the trip home. He sets off in a boat in order to throw his instruments into the sea, gets lost, and is eventually washed ashore in Ireland. He is immediately arrested in connection with a murder.

COMMENTARY

Although Victor speaks of the '**sophisms**', the false but persuasive arguments of the monster, his own reasoning here seems equally sophistical: he is seeking for excuses not to honour his promise. When the monster later murders Elizabeth, it could be said that he is only doing what Victor has already done to him in destroying the female. The threat, 'I shall be with you on your wedding-night,' suggests that Victor will then be unable to avoid a confrontation with his sexuality.

CHAPTER 21

- The murdered man is Clerval.
- Victor is imprisoned.
- His father arrives.
- He is released.

Taken before the magistrate, Victor hears that a body of a young man had been found on the shore with black finger marks on his neck. Remembering the murder of William, Victor becomes agitated, arousing the suspicions of the magistrate further. He is taken to see the corpse and is horrified to find it is Clerval. Victor is carried out of the room in convulsions and spends two months in a fever, confessing to the murders of William, Justine and Clerval in his delirium. The kindly magistrate does his best for Victor and brings Alphonse Frankenstein to Ireland. Victor is eventually acquitted. Full of remorse and guilt, he cannot, however, enjoy his freedom. He determines to watch over his family in Geneva and lie in wait for the next appearance of the monster.

COMMENTARY

In confessing to the murders in his delirium, Victor once more associates himself with the monster. He is both physically and mentally ill, and the horrific nightmares that haunt him also suggest that the horror is in his psyche.

GLOSSARY

182	*maladie du pays*	homesickness
183	Havre-de-Grace	original name of the French port of Le Havre

CHAPTER 22

- Frankenstein returns to Geneva.
- He marries Elizabeth.
- They journey to Lake Como.

The journey home begins. Victor shuns all society and his insistence that he is the assassin convinces his father that he is deranged. He receives a letter from Elizabeth, wondering if he regrets being bound to marry her. The letter revives the memory of the monster's threat to be with him on his wedding night. Victor, assuming this means that he will be killed then, determines nevertheless to give Elizabeth what happiness he can. He writes to reassure her of his love and intentions, tells her there is a terrible secret he will reveal to her when they are married, and returns to Geneva. They are married and start the journey to Lake Como for their honeymoon. The first evening they proceed as far as Lake Geneva.

CONTEXT

The Sophists were a professional class of teachers who wandered around Greece around the fifth century BC. As the most popular career choice at the time was politics, the sophists focused mainly on rhetoric and had a stock of arguments on a wide range of issues designed to prove any position. A sophism is now defined as a subtle and deceptive method of reasoning or arguing, involving statements that sound plausible but are actually false.

CONTEXT

Lake Como is in northern Italy, twenty-five miles northeast of Milan, and known for its beauty. The Shelleys first visited the lake in the spring of 1818 and Mary Shelley returned during the summer of 1840 for a lengthy visit that she recorded in her *Rambles in Germany and Italy*, 1844.

CHECK THE BOOK

Interesting accounts of Shelley's own travels can be found in her journals. See Paula R. Feldman and Diana Scott-Kilvert eds., *The Journals of Mary Shelley, 1814–1844*, 1987.

CHECK THE BOOK

For a general exploration of representation and conceptions of monstrosity through the ages, see Jeffrey Jerome Cohen's *Monster Theory. Reading Culture*, 1996.

COMMENTARY

Since it is quite clear to the reader that the monster's threat was directed towards Elizabeth, Victor seems rather obtuse in interpreting it as being directed towards him. The reference to 'paradisiacal dreams' (p. 189) indicates that now Victor is seeing himself as Adam, and Elizabeth as his Paradise. But having already drunk too deeply of forbidden knowledge, with the apple already eaten, he knows his Paradise is lost to him. The chapter ends with a description of the beauties of nature from which Victor is now excluded.

GLOSSARY		
186	**sea of ice**	the glacier Mer de Glace
191	**nicer**	more perceptive
191	**decorations**	used in archaic sense to refer to scenery on stage
192	**artifice**	trickery
192	**Evian**	resort on Lake Geneva

CHAPTER 23

- Elizabeth is murdered by the monster.
- Victor determines on revenge.

As night falls, and the calm gives way to a fearful storm, Victor is increasingly agitated and Elizabeth questions him. 'Oh! peace, peace, my love,' he responds, 'this night, and all will be safe: but this night is dreadful, very dreadful' (p. 194). Anticipating combat with the monster, Victor sends Elizabeth to their room. Suddenly he hears a dreadful scream; he rushes to the room to find his wife's lifeless form 'flung by the murderer on its bridal bier' (p. 195). Victor faints. When he recovers he sees the grinning face of the monster at the window, pointing towards the corpse. Victor resolves to return to Geneva, fearing that his remaining family are under threat.

His father, heartbroken at the news, dies. Victor spends some time in a mental asylum and upon his release determines upon revenge. He tells his strange story to a magistrate who is incredulous; he claims to believe the story, but refuses to take any action. Victor, enraged, denounces him: 'Man,' he cries, 'how ignorant art thou in thy pride of wisdom! Cease; you know not what it is you say' (p. 201). The words could equally serve as his own epitaph.

COMMENTARY

The storm heralds the imminent arrival of the monster, and the wedding night scene makes particularly clear Victor's horror of natural sexuality. His comforting words to Elizabeth may be read as his repulsion at the thought of the now apparently unavoidable consummation of their marriage. Leaving Elizabeth alone in the room, ostensibly to draw the monster's rage away from her, he actually leaves her open to attack. The language used to describe the appearance of the monster at the window, pointing towards the corpse of Elizabeth, echoes the language used to describe that dreary night when he was created, linking death and birth again, taking us back to the nightmare that followed. The fears suggested by that nightmare have now been actualised.

GLOSSARY	
195	**bier** where a corpse is laid before burial
197	**acme** culmination or highest point

CHAPTER 24

- Victor pursues the monster.
- Walton continues the story.
- His sailors desire to return home.
- Victor dies.
- Walton talks with the monster.
- The monster departs.

 CHECK THE NET

The scene of Elizabeth's death may well be inspired by a painting by Henry Fuseli called 'The Nightmare'; see the image at **http:// www.dia.org/ collections/ euroart/romantic/ 55.5.a.html**. The first of several versions of *The Nightmare* was exhibited at the Royal Academy in 1782. It depicts a woman stretched out across a bed sleeping, the covers thrown off, and her arms flung up over her head. On her torso crouches an incubus, and peering through the curtain is a horse, the 'nightmare' of the title, with its eyes gleaming and its teeth bared. The painting, increasingly erotic as the different versions progressed, suggests both terror and a vague sense of oppression.

Victor's narrative concludes during the course of this long chapter. He describes a visit to the cemetery where the murdered members of his family lie. Here, in a highly theatrical moment, he voices aloud his determination on revenge. An answering laugh echoes through the mountains and he hears a whisper in his ear: 'I am satisfied: miserable wretch! you have determined to live, and I am satisfied' (p. 203). Victor begins his pursuit of the monster, following him to the Black Sea and then on to Tartary and Russia. Victor's account of what he now refers to as his 'pilgrimage' (p. 204) concludes with his desperate condition when he, marooned on an ice-raft, finally sees Walton's ship. He asks Walton to swear that, if he should die, Walton should, if the opportunity presented itself, kill the monster.

Walton continues the story in a series of letters to Margaret. He expresses both pity and admiration for Victor: 'What a glorious creature must he have been in the days of his prosperity, when he is thus noble and godlike in ruin!' (p. 210). Victor spurns both Walton's offer of friendship and his attempts to reconcile him with life; all he desires now is to destroy the monster.

In the meantime, it appears as though Walton's ship will be destroyed by the encroaching ice, and he fears a mutiny from the despairing crew. The sailors eventually demand to return home. Victor gives a stirring speech, adjuring them to remain steady and firm to their purpose: 'Oh! be men, or be more than men' (p. 215). The sailors are moved, but still demand the promise from Walton, and he, disappointed, gives it.

The last letter concludes both the chapter and the book. He affirms his belief in the need to destroy the monster and begs Walton to take on his quest; as he speaks, he dies. Later, Walton finds the monster bending over Victor, full of grief, horror and self-reproach. To Walton's recriminations, he responds with an explanation of the anguish he endured. Comparing himself once again to Milton's Satan, he explains: 'Evil thenceforth became my good.' (p. 220) He has come to hate himself, but continues to insist on the injustices he suffered: 'I, the miserable and the abandoned, am an abortion, to be spurned at, and kicked, and trampled on' (p. 222). With the

CHECK THE BOOK

Mary Shelley's own letters can be read in Betty T. Bennett, ed., *The Letters of Mary Wollstonecraft Shelley*, 1988.

CONTEXT

Percy Shelley died shortly before his thirtieth birthday in a boating accident in the bay of La Spezia in July of 1822; after his body was washed up on shore ten days later, his friends, including Byron, decided to send him out in style with a dramatic funeral pyre on the beach that somewhat uncannily duplicates the monster's proposed ending.

intention of immolating himself on a funeral pyre, the monster springs from the cabin window and soon becomes 'lost in darkness and distance' (p. 223). On this bleak note, the novel ends.

COMMENTARY

Rather strangely, considering what Victor has done to him, the monster still admires and esteems his creator and is full of remorse for what he has done to this great man. His attitude to Victor echoes that of Walton. The sailors also respond to Victor in a similar manner. Does Shelley convince us that Victor's character justifies such excessive adoration?

Both Victor and the monster in this chapter lay claim to a resemblance to Milton's Satan, and in so doing they vie with each other to claim the most suffering; Satan, in *Paradise Lost*, is noted above all for being the most miserable of all beings.

The monster's final speech emphasises the fact that his monstrousness is no different from that of society. His plan for his solitary death, a blazing fire amongst the icy wastes, is a **parody** of Walton's dream of finding a tropical paradise at the pole, and also reminiscent of Victor's attempt to animate a cold corpse with the fire of life. Such quests, such dreams, Shelley seems to suggest, can only end with destruction.

> **? QUESTION**
>
> What is the significance of the landscape that dominates the novel's final scenes?

GLOSSARY

202	the furies possessed me the furies were Graeco-Roman goddesses of vengeance, sent to punish men for their crimes; they were particularly concerned with those who neglected family duties
205	The Greeks wept for joy Xenophon (431–c.350BC) records this in Anabasis, when he describes leading the Greek soldiers out of Asia in 400BC
209	manes spirits of the dead
211	projectors promoters of speculative schemes
216	a composing draught a sedative
220	Evil thenceforth became my good Paradise Lost, 4.108–10: 'Evil, be thou my good'

EXTENDED COMMENTARIES

TEXT 1 (PAGES 57–8)

It was on a dreary night of November, that I beheld the accomplishment of my toils. With an anxiety that almost amounted to agony, I collected the instruments of life around me, that I might infuse a spark of being into the lifeless thing that lay at my feet. It was already one in the morning; the rain pattered dismally against the panes, and my candle was nearly burnt out, when, by the glimmer of the half-extinguished light, I saw the dull yellow eye of the creature open; it breathed hard, and a convulsive motion agitated its limbs.

How can I describe my emotions at this catastrophe, or how delineate the wretch whom with such infinite pains and care I had endeavoured to form? His limbs were in proportion, and I had selected his features as beautiful. Beautiful! – Great God! His yellow skin scarcely covered the work of muscles and arteries beneath; his hair was of a lustrous black, and flowing; his teeth of a pearly whiteness; but these luxuriances only formed a more horrid contrast with his watery eyes, that seemed almost of the same colour as the dun white sockets in which they were set, his shrivelled complexion and straight black lips.

The different accidents of life are not so changeable as the feelings of human nature. I had worked hard for nearly two years, for the sole purpose of infusing life into an inanimate body. For this I had deprived myself of rest and health. I had desired it with an ardour that far exceeded moderation; but now that I had finished, the beauty of the dream vanished, and breathless horror and disgust filled my heart. Unable to endure the aspect of the being I had created, I rushed out of the room, and continued a long time traversing my bedchamber, unable to compose my mind to sleep. At length lassitude succeeded to the tumult I had before endured; and I threw myself on the bed in my clothes, endeavouring to seek a few moments of forgetfulness. But it was in vain: I slept, indeed, but I was disturbed by the wildest dreams. I thought I saw Elizabeth, in the bloom of health, walking in the streets of Ingolstadt. Delighted and surprised, I embraced her; but as I imprinted the

CHECK THE FILM

In Shelley's novel, Frankenstein works alone in his isolated laboratory; in James Whale's classic film, monster-making is a collective activity, with audience in place and assistant at hand. For a discussion of this and other changes in Whale's film, and how these help us understand the original text, see **http://www.rc. umd.edu/praxis/ frankenstein** and search for Marc Redfield's on-line essay, 'Frankenstein's Cinematic Dream'.

first kiss on her lips, they became livid with the hue of death; her features appeared to change, and I thought that I held the corpse of my dead mother in my arms; a shroud enveloped her form, and I saw the grave-worms crawling in the folds of the flannel. I started from my sleep with horror; a cold dew covered my forehead, my teeth chattered, and every limb became convulsed: when, by the dim and yellow light of the moon, as it forced its way through the window shutters, I beheld the wretch – the miserable monster whom I had created. He held up the curtain of the bed; and his eyes, if eyes they may be called, were fixed on me. His jaws opened, and he muttered some inarticulate sounds, while a grin wrinkled his cheeks. He might have spoken, but I did not hear; one hand was stretched out, seemingly to detain me, but I escaped, and rushed down stairs. I took refuge in the courtyard belonging to the house which I inhabited; where I remained during the rest of the night, walking up and down in the greatest agitation, listening attentively, catching and fearing each sound as if it were to announce the approach of the demoniacal corpse to which I had so miserably given life.

In this passage we arrive at a climax of horror as Victor describes the moment he has anticipated with increasing anxiety for two years. In much the same manner as the mythic Prometheus animates the man he formed of clay, Victor finally animates the creature that he has constructed out of the fragments of corpses, using the 'spark' of life. While Shelley is not clear about how this is accomplished, her description of Darwin's experiments in the 1831 Introduction, along with Victor's early interests, encourage us to deduce that the 'spark' (p. 57) of life for this modern Prometheus is not fire, but electricity: this would certainly fit with the novel's general concern with contemporary scientific developments.

The agony of expectation Victor is experiencing at the opening of this passage, the intensity of his feelings, contrast tellingly with the **atmosphere** of dull misery and dreariness that Shelley creates. When he later becomes determined on revenge, the imminent appearance of the monster is often heralded by thunder and lightning. The actual moment of his animation is set on a dull and 'dreary' night in November. The rain patters 'dismally' (p. 57); the

 CHECK THE NET

For a discussion of the dreams in *Frankenstein* read, Jerrold E. Hogle's 'Frankenstein's Dream: An Introduction'. This can be found in an excellent on-line journal in the Romantic Circles Praxis Series: **http://www.rc. umd.edu/praxis/ frankenstein/**.

candle is only just glimmering. There is little sense of 'animation' (p. 59) here. It is an appropriately bleak and depressing scene for the opening of the 'dull yellow eye' (p. 57) of the creature Victor so repeatedly describes as 'miserable' (p. 58) and the cause of his misery.

If we read *Frankenstein* as a birth myth, then this is the moment when Victor gives 'birth'. Some critics have argued that the description of the newly animated monster is suggestive of a newborn child, frequently jaundiced, misshapen, shrivelled, and often a great disappointment to the unprepared parent. Whether we accept this or not, Victor has certainly just created life, produced a child, and he has, significantly, circumvented the normal channels of procreation.

He is immediately horrified by the 'wretch' (pp. 57 and 58) he has created; this is not a triumph but a 'catastrophe'. 'I had selected his features as beautiful,' Victor tells us, and then exclaims in horror: 'Beautiful! – Great God!' (p. 57). Victor, like all who encounter the creature, is repelled by and unable to look beyond the physical ugliness, the alien appearance. Shelley offers a criticism of an intolerant and superficial society that places so much emphasis on the importance of physical beauty, the importance of not deviating from the norm. That which is ugly or alien is always rejected as monstrous: the exterior is assumed to reflect the inner being. Even little William has already absorbed the prejudices of society and reacts to the creature in as much horror as his brother. Victor's first act, then, is to reject and abandon his child.

QUESTION

In what ways might it be possible to argue that Shelley is actually equating the beautiful with the good rather than criticising this tendency? Begin by thinking of Elizabeth.

Victor runs away, as he so often tries to run away from troubles, and attempts to forget in sleep. This sleep, however, is disturbed by the 'wildest dreams' (p. 58). He awakens with a start, displaying all the physical manifestations of fear: his forehead is covered with 'a cold dew' and his teeth chatter. The language here, and in particular the reference to Victor's 'limbs' which 'convulsed' (p. 58) is in some ways reminiscent of the language used to describe the creature coming to life, when 'a convulsive motion agitated its limbs' (p. 57). This may be the first indication that the monster is Victor's **double**. Immediately, 'by the dim and yellow light of the moon', he sees the 'miserable' monster bent over him (p. 58). This is the first of three occasions when Victor sees the monster by moonlight. The next time will be when he destroys the female creature, and the last time when the monster, in retaliation, murders Elizabeth. The monster, then, through the repetition of this visual image, is at the moment of birth immediately linked to death, in particular, to the death of the female.

To the reader, the description of the monster on this particular occasion seems full of pathos. He tries to communicate, muttering 'inarticulate' (p. 58) sounds as he grins at his creator. The first things he desires are contact and affection, and these remain his primary needs. He stretches out one arm towards Victor. This could be a **parody** of Michelangelo's *The Creation of Man* in the Sistine Chapel, suggesting an **analogy** between Victor and God and the monster and Adam, and anticipating the many **allusions** to Milton's *Paradise Lost* which subsequently play an important role in shaping the development of the characters. Though we may see something touching in the creature's desire to reach out to his maker, Victor again simply runs away in horror. He appears to find the monster a threat, and he 'escapes'. Victor repeatedly misinterprets the creature's expressions, seeing aggression where we see pleasure, affection, or a desire to please. He is not, therefore, the most reliable of **narrators**.

CHECK THE NET

See a reproduction of Michelangelo's *The Creation of Man* at **http:// www. webcolombia.com /michelangelo/**.

In juxtaposing Victor's dream with this vision of the monster, Shelley encourages us to consider the possible connections between dream and reality and opens up several possible layers of interpretation. The dream may suggest that to bring the monster to life is equivalent to killing Elizabeth, and in this way the dream is prophetic. This does not, however, account for Elizabeth changing into the corpse of his dead mother. The reason for this becomes clearer when we consider that Victor has just given 'birth' by himself and circumvented the normal channels of procreation, usurped the role of woman, made her unnecessary. His dream then also appears to suggest that the fulfilment of Victor's 'dream' of finding the secret of life has effectively 'killed' the mother.

These two interpretations indicate the potential results of the creation of the monster. We might also consider, however, what the

CONTEXT

From a psychoanalytical perspective, the Gothic can be said to deal with the return of the repressed, with subconscious energies bursting out from the restraints of the conscious ego. All those things we push away, out of consciousness, in the process of constructing ourselves as civilised beings, come back to the surface. The dream becomes an important part of Gothic as the dream can be said to participate in this disruption and violation of our 'realities', revealing repressed desires and anxieties in much the same way.

dream implies about the dreamer himself. Dreams allow things normally kept buried and repressed to come to the surface; these might be socially unacceptable desires or feelings which we are unable to face. When Victor attempts to kiss Elizabeth she turns into a corpse. This suggests that sexuality revolts and frightens Victor; he associates it with death. He would prefer to find a means of procreation that eliminated sexual activity. If his monster is read as an expression of his sexuality, then it is inevitable that the monster should kill Elizabeth on the wedding night, the moment when Victor can no longer avoid facing up to his sexuality. Since Elizabeth transforms into the corpse of his mother, it is possible to deduce that one of the things which frightens Victor most about his 'monstrous' sexuality is that it includes incestuous desires. The dream reveals what he cannot face, cannot express.

This passage is of particular interest because it allows us to come to some conclusions concerning the nature of Victor's crime. The original Prometheus was punished for presuming to usurp the role of God and create life. This modern Prometheus appears to be punished more for his rejection and abandonment of his creation. Here we are offered various readings of the relationship between creator and creation. We can see Victor as the father figure, the monster as child. Victor might be a new Prometheus, the creature the new man. Victor could also be placed in the role of God, and the monster his Adam. We can also, however, see the monster as the embodiment of Victor's sexuality, sexuality which he sees as horrific, perverse, and destructive. If it is this which he rejects in horror and represses, then it is inevitable that these sexual desires will not remain buried and ignored. They will emerge with a violent destructive force. The passage therefore also provides us with some insight into the nature of terror. Real terror, Shelley suggests, is not a reaction to such physical entities as monsters, ghosts, or vampires. Real terror is a reaction to what these things suggest lies lurking within the darkest corners of our minds.

TEXT 2 (PAGES 98–100)

As I said this, I suddenly beheld the figure of a man, at some distance, advancing towards me with superhuman speed. He bounded over the crevices in the ice, among which I had walked with caution; his stature, also, as he approached, seemed to exceed that of a man. I was troubled; a mist came over my eyes, and I felt a faintness seize me; but I was quickly restored by the cold gale of the mountains. I perceived, as the shape came nearer (sight tremendous and abhorred?) that it was the wretch whom I had created. I trembled with rage and horror, resolving to wait his approach, and then close with him in mortal combat. He approached; his countenance bespoke bitter anguish, combined with disdain and malignity, while its unearthly ugliness rendered it almost too horrible for human eyes. But I scarcely observed this; rage and hatred had at first deprived me of utterance, and I recovered only to overwhelm him with words expressive of furious detestation and contempt.

'Devil,' I exclaimed, 'do you dare approach me? and do not you fear the fierce vengeance of my arm wreaked on your miserable head? Begone, vile insect! or rather, stay, that I may trample you to dust! and, oh! that I could, with the extinction of your miserable existence, restore those victims whom you have so diabolically murdered!'

'I expected this reception,' said the daemon. 'All men hate the wretched; how, then, must I be hated, who am miserable beyond all living things! Yet you, my creator, detest and spurn me, thy creature, to whom thou art bound by ties only dissoluble by the annihilation of one of us. You purpose to kill me. How dare you sport thus with life? Do your duty towards me, and I will do mine towards you and the rest of mankind. If you will comply with my conditions, I will leave them and you at peace; but if you refuse, I will glut the maw of death, until it be satiated with the blood of your remaining friends.'

'Abhorred monster! fiend that thou art! the tortures of hell are too mild a vengeance for thy crimes. Wretched devil! you reproach me with your creation; come on, then, that I may extinguish the spark which I so negligently bestowed.'

My rage was without bounds; I sprang on him, impelled by all the feelings which can arm one being against the existence of another.

He easily eluded me, and said –

CHECK THE BOOK

James Heffernan's 'Looking at the Monster: *Frankenstein* and Film', *Critical Inquiry* 24.1 ,1997, considers what film versions can tell us about the role of the visual in the life of the monster in the original text.

QUESTION

Does *Frankenstein* as a whole confirm the monster's assumption that happiness creates virtue?

'Be calm! I entreat you to hear me, before you give vent to your hatred on my devoted head. Have I not suffered enough, that you seek to increase my misery? Life, although it may only be an accumulation of anguish, is dear to me, and I will defend it. Remember, thou has made me more powerful than thyself; my height is superior to thine; my joints more supple. But I will not be tempted to set myself in opposition to thee. I am thy creature, and I will be even mild and docile to my natural lord and king, if thou wilt also perform thy part, the which thou owest me. Oh, Frankenstein, be not equitable to every other, and trample upon me alone, to whom thy justice, and even thy clemency and affection, is most due. Remember, that I am thy creature; I ought to be thy Adam; but I am rather the fallen angel, whom thou drivest from joy for no misdeed. Every where I see bliss, from which I alone am irrevocably excluded. I was benevolent and good; misery made me a fiend. Make me happy, and I shall again be virtuous.'

Tormented by guilt and rage following the deaths of William and Justine, Victor goes to the valley of Chamo[u]nix in an attempt to forget his sorrows in the magnificence of nature. On the day of his arrival, he does indeed find comfort amongst the **sublime** and magnificent scenery. The passage in question describes the contrasting scene on the summit of Montanvert the following day. All has now changed. A storm heralds the imminent arrival of the monster, and nature seems violent and terrifying. Victor sees a large and agile form bounding over the crevices with 'superhuman' (p. 98) speed and knows what he must now face. Unable to respond in his usual manner to the monster and what he represents, unable, that is, to run away or fall asleep, Victor almost faints. This escape too is denied him by a cold blast of wind. He is forced to accept a confrontation with his monster and resolves to kill him.

The exchange between Victor and the creature is of particular interest for the various shifts in roles that take place. An examination of language reveals the first of these. The creature's language is generally calm and reasoned, biblically solemn and dignified. He is an eloquent **rhetorician**. He draws with skill upon such devices as **oxymoron** and **antitheses**: 'I ought to be thy Adam, but I am rather the fallen angel' (p. 100). His most terrifying threats are expressed with elegantly constructed phrases: 'If you will comply with my conditions, I will leave them and you at peace; but if you refuse, I will glut the maw of death, until it be satiated with the blood of your remaining friends' (p. 99). **Parallelism** and repetition here produce, in contrast to the terrible violence threatened, a harmonious arrangement of words, suggestive of balance and reasoning. This is the first time we hear the monster speak, and we may have been expecting only grunts. What we find, however, is that despite his hideous appearance, he is the most eloquent character in the novel; there is a striking contradiction here between the verbal and the visual. The source of his eloquence and analogies only later becomes clear when we learn about his education and the impressive reading list that includes *Paradise Lost*.

In comparison, Victor seems to do little more than splutter insults and threats. His language clearly reveals that he is in the grip of a terrible savage passion, and, of course, this is understandable. But he is ultimately only diminished by this passion. His speeches are almost absurdly **melodramatic**, full of exclamations, of such theatrical expressions as 'Begone, vile insect!' He addresses the creature like the vengeful God of the Old Testament: 'do not you fear the fierce vengeance of my arm wreaked on your miserable head?' (p. 99). Victor repeatedly refers to the violence of his feelings: his rage is 'without bounds'; he 'trembled with rage and horror' (p. 99); 'rage and hatred' at first deprive him of speech, but then he overwhelms the monster with words 'expressive of furious detestation and contempt' (p.99). For all Victor's threats, these words convey little more than a sense of flailing impotence. This is further emphasised by the constant reminders of the superior physical strength and agility of the monster; as he reminds Victor: 'thou hast made me more powerful than thyself' (p.100). When Victor springs upon him in rage, he can easily elude his creator's grasp. Victor may call him an 'insect' (p. 99), but, considering the power and size of the monster, the image could be more appropriately applied to Victor himself. Victor claims to detect 'disdain and malignity' (p. 99) in the creature's countenance. In this passage, however, the boundaries between the human and the monstrous seem to dissolve as Victor's savage passions suggest that he, not the apparently more civilised creature, is the true monster.

> **CONTEXT**
>
> While the word melodrama is commonly used to describe anything that relies heavily on the sensational, violent or improbable, the term originally referred to a play with music and encompassed early opera. These plays were usually with simple characters and much violent action.

CHECK THE BOOK

The relationship between Victor Frankenstein and his creature is represented in various different ways in the film versions. One of the most interesting books in this respect is Steven Earl Forry's *Hideous Progenies: Dramatizations of Frankenstein from Mary Shelley to the Present*, 1990.

CHECK THE NET

For a useful summary of William Godwin's works and ideas, see **http://www. historyguide.org/ intellect/godwin. html**.

Variously employing such **epithets** as 'devil', 'daemon', and 'fiend' (p. 99), Victor also places the monster in the role of Satan, claiming the torments of hell are not a sufficient punishment for his crimes. The monster agrees with the **analogy**, but presents it in quite a different light when he describes his miserable condition. Three times in this passage he reminds Victor 'I am thy creature' (p. 100). He should be Adam to Victor's God, but 'am rather the fallen angel' (p. 100). He has been transformed into this 'fallen angel' not through any fault of his own, but because Victor has made him, like Satan, the most miserable of beings. Despite his power and size, the creature believes Victor, as his creator, is still his 'natural lord and king' (p. 100). He describes himself as 'devoted' (p. 99) and is quite willing to be submissive. He insists only that if he is to play his natural and proper role, to be 'mild and docile' (p. 100) to his lord, then Victor must too play his natural and proper role and not simply reject and abandon him. It is only much later, when Victor destroys his last hope by tearing apart the female, that the monster abandons his belief in these roles. Addressing Victor as 'Slave', he then assumes authority: 'You are my creator, but I am your master; – obey!' (p. 167).

Echoing William Godwin's belief that man's natural emotions were those of benevolence, affection, and pity, Shelley has her monster, her natural man or new Adam, claim that he was instinctively 'benevolent and good' (p. 100). What the monster desires is what Victor rejects: love and companionship. While Victor chooses his own isolation, it is forced upon the monster and his resulting misery makes him 'a fiend' (p. 100). Shelley suggests that it is natural to long for affection, and that in this respect, again, it is Victor, not the creature, who is abnormal. Through the repeated blurring of roles in this passage, the undermining of all our assumptions and expectations, Shelley problematises the very notion of the human and the monstrous.

TEXT 3 (PAGES 142–4)

At this time a slight sleep relieved me from the pain of reflection, which was disturbed by the approach of a beautiful child, who came running into the recess I had chosen, with all the sportiveness of infancy. Suddenly, as I gazed on him, an idea seized me, that this little creature was unprejudiced, and had lived too short a time to have imbibed a horror of my deformity. If, therefore, I could seize him, and educate him as my companion and friend, I should not be so desolate in this peopled earth.

Urged by this impulse, I seized on the boy as he passed, and drew him towards me. As soon as he beheld my form, he placed his hands before his eyes, and uttered a shrill scream: I drew his hand forcibly from his face, and said, 'Child, what is the meaning of this? I do not intend to hurt you; listen to me.'

He struggled violently. 'Let me go,' he cried; 'monster! ugly wretch! you wish to eat me, and tear me to pieces – You are an ogre – Let me go, or I will tell my papa.'

'Boy, you will never see your father again; you must come with me.'

'Hideous monster! let me go. My papa is a Syndic – he is M. Frankenstein – he will punish you. You dare not keep me.'

'Frankenstein! you belong then to my enemy – to him towards whom I have sworn eternal revenge; you shall be my first victim.'

The child still struggled, and loaded me with epithets which carried despair to my heart; I grasped his throat to silence him, and in a moment he lay dead at my feet. I gazed on my victim, and my heart swelled with exultation and hellish triumph: clapping my hands, I exclaimed, 'I, too, can create desolation; my enemy is not invulnerable: this death will carry despair to him, and a thousand other miseries shall torment and destroy him.'

As I fixed my eyes on the child, I saw something glittering on his breast. I took it; it was a portrait of a most lovely woman. In spite of my malignity, it softened and attracted me. For a few moments I gazed with delight on her dark eyes, fringed by deep lashes, and her lovely lips; but presently my rage returned: I remembered that I was for ever deprived of the delights that such beautiful creatures could bestow; and that she whose resemblance I contemplated would, in regarding me, have changed that air of divine benignity to one expressive of disgust and affright.

CONTEXT

Representations and inter-pretations of monstrosity change over time. Shelley's novel is perhaps the first to invite sympathy for the monster, but it is often suggested that in recent times the monstrous has increasingly become a site of identification for the reader rather than a demonic force to be expelled. Can you think of any examples of this from, say, vampire fiction?

CHECK THE FILM

Kenneth Branagh's *Mary Shelley's Frankenstein*, 1994, makes a significant change to the episode of William's murder. Justine is not arrested and put to trial, but immediately lynched by an angry mob while Victor Frankenstein and Elizabeth look on helplessly. Consider how this changes our response to the character of Frankenstein who, at this stage in the film, does not know the monster is alive and the murderer.

CHECK THE NET

For a guide to internet resources on Mary Shelley, see **http://www.ucalgary.ca/UofC/Others/CIH/WritingLives/WLMSlinks.html**.

Can you wonder that such thoughts transported me with rage? I only wonder that at that moment, instead of venting my sensations in exclamations and agony, I did not rush among mankind, and perish in the attempt to destroy them.

While I was overcome by these feelings, I left the spot where I had committed the murder, and seeking a more secluded hiding-place, I entered a barn which had appeared to me to be empty. A woman was sleeping on some straw; she was young: not indeed so beautiful as her whose portrait I held; but of an agreeable aspect, and blooming in the loveliness of youth and health. Here, I thought, is one of those whose joy-imparting smiles are bestowed upon all but me. And then I bent over her, and whispered, 'Awake, fairest, thy lover is near – he who would give his life but to obtain one look of affection from thine eyes: my beloved, awake!'

The sleeper stirred; a thrill of terror ran through me. Should she indeed awake, and see me, and curse me, and denounce the murderer? Thus would she assuredly act, if her darkened eyes opened, and she beheld me. The thought was madness; it stirred the fiend within me – not I, but she shall suffer: the murder I have committed because I am for ever robbed of all that she could give me, she shall atone. The crime had its source in her: be hers the punishment! Thanks to the lessons of Felix and the sanguinary laws of man, I had learned now to work mischief. I bent over her, and placed the portrait securely in one of the folds of her dress. She moved again, and I fled.

This passage places us in the innermost embedded narrative of *Frankenstein*. The monster is reaching the conclusion of the story he tells Victor, whose own narrative serves to frame that of the monster. He recalls how, after being rejected by the De Laceys and shot by a villager whose child he saved from drowning, he finally determined on revenge for the injustice he has suffered. In focusing upon the creature's first murder, the moment when he becomes truly demonic, Shelley encourages us to consider how our personalities are formed and what forces can transform a man into a monster.

The passage begins as the monster is disturbed from sleep by the arrival of little William. He sees 'a beautiful child, who came running to the recess I had chosen, with all the sportiveness of infancy' (p. 142). The syntax could momentarily confuse us. It may initially seem as though the 'sportiveness of infancy' could refer to either William or the monster; it soon becomes clear, however, that both these 'children' have lost the wonder and innocence associated with the phrase. They have learned the lessons of society too well.

The monster wavers at the sight of William; his destructive impulses are momentarily buried again as he assumes that this little creature must be as yet 'unprejudiced' (p. 142) and therefore could be educated to be his companion and friend. The child, however, has already been socialised through the tales he has been told about 'ogres' and 'monsters'. He has learned to abhor and fear anything that is alien and different. William displays just the same horror at the sight of the monster as all the others, even using one of Victor's favourite **epithets**: 'wretch' (p. 142). The scene may be said both to **parallel** and reverse the previous encounter with Felix. Like Felix, William simply assumes ugliness means threat and does not understand the real intentions of the monster. 'I do not intend to hurt you; listen to me' (p. 142), the monster says. While language has the power to hurt the monster, who is filled with despair by the epithets used by the child, language has no power to check the overwhelming force of prejudice provoked by the visually alien. While Felix tries to protect his father from the threat, William invokes his father to protect him.

By this time, our sympathies have been completely transferred to the monster; William seems like a nasty and spoilt little boy. It is precisely at this moment, however, that the monster becomes truly demonic. When William utters the name of Frankenstein, the monster's desire for revenge again surfaces and he strangles the child. He is now indeed Satanic, his heart fills with 'hellish triumph' (p. 143), and he becomes increasingly Satanic as this passage develops. He realises he can make Victor as desolate as he has made him. In many ways this passage lends itself to a Freudian reading, and the monster can be seen as acting out a displaced **Oedipal conflict**, that is, the repressed but continuing presence in the man's

QUESTION

Compare Shelley's attitude to the child here with the most famous Romantic lament for the loss of childhood radiance, Wordsworth's 'Ode: Intimations of Immortality from Recollections of Early Childhood'.

unconscious of the desire to possess the mother and destroy the father. Here, the monster displaces his aggression towards the father on to the son who invokes his name.

At the very moment the monster appears most horrific, he sees the miniature of Caroline. Women in this novel are notable primarily for their effect on others; Elizabeth, for example, has previously been called 'the living spirit of love to soften and attract' (p. 38). Caroline has a similar influence, even through the medium of her portrait. As he gazes on her loveliness, the monster finds that in spite of his malignity, 'it softened and attracted me' (p. 143). The response of little William, however, has settled one issue conclusively: no one, no matter how apparently innocent or gentle, will respond to the monster with kindness or affection. Remembering he is excluded by his ugliness from the delights women could bestow, the monster is again filled with rage and agony.

CONTEXT

Mary Shelley's mother, Mary Wollstonecraft, died ten days after giving birth of post-natal septicaemia.

We know, although the monster does not, that this is Victor's mother. Mothers in *Frankenstein*, as in most of Shelley's works, are notable mainly for their absence; they indicate a lack or a gap, something which is desired but prohibited. This is particularly true in the case of the monster, whose erotic gaze is fixed on the maternal figure that he, due to the circumstances of his birth, has been denied. This lack and this desire may be of particular significance if we consider the monster as Victor's **double**. Victor too has been denied his mother through death, and his fear of the sexuality which he sees as horrific is at least partly a fear of his incestuous desires. He longs for the mother, but also fears and hates her because he cannot possess her.

Soon after, the monster encounters Justine. The desire he has felt in gazing at the portrait is transferred to the woman he finds sleeping at his feet. While this scene has been described as a perverse fantasy of rape, there is far more tenderness than violence in the monster's language. Echoing Satan whispering seductively into the ear of the sleeping Eve in Milton's *Paradise Lost*, he whispers to Justine: 'Awake, fairest, thy lover is near' (p. 143). His attempt at seduction is halted, however, by the recollection that if Justine should awake she would denounce him as a murderer. All his satanic impulses now come to the fore: the 'fiend' (p. 144) stirs within him. The hostility he feels at being denied possession of the mother is transferred to this mother substitute, 'not indeed so beautiful as her whose portrait I held; but of an agreeable aspect' (p. 143). He decides to implicate Justine in the murder, condemns her because he cannot possess her.

As the monster notes, he is no longer an innocent. The treatment he has received from others has provided him with a good education in cruelty and injustice. 'The crime', he declares, 'had its source in her; be hers the punishment!' (p. 144). This is a strange claim and perhaps understandable only if, again, we see the monster as Victor's double, acting out Victor's aggression towards women, and, in particular, see the monster as an embodiment of Victor's horrific sexuality, where the mother is desired but prohibited, and where the erotic is fused with the murderous.

This passage, then, lends itself to two quite different interpretations. If we read the passage from a sociological perspective, we might conclude that Shelley provides us with a critique of society and human injustice and an analysis of how our initially benevolent natures can be perverted through socialisation. If we read from a psychological perspective, however, we might see Shelley as anticipating some of Freud's theories, and showing the monster/Victor to be acting out a displaced Oedipal complex. These two readings exist quite happily side by side, and Shelley seems to be suggesting that it is both the external forces that act upon us and the inner workings of the psyche that turn 'men' into 'monsters'.

> **CONTEXT**
>
> One influence on both the Shelleys was the philosopher and novelist Jean-Jacques Rousseau (1712-78). His works include *Emile,* or *De l'education,*1762, which advocates an education in which the child was to be free and to learn by making mistakes. The unpopularity of this work led to his banishment from France.

PART THREE

CRITICAL APPROACHES

CHARACTERISATION

VICTOR FRANKENSTEIN

CHECK THE NET

For a discussion of *Frankenstein* in the context of cyborgs and technology, search for Robert W. Anderson's 'Body Parts that Matter: Frankenstein, or the Modern Cyborg?'.

CHECK THE BOOK

A useful article that addresses Shelley's reworking of Romanticism and the Romantic hero is Mary Poovey's '"My Hideous Progeny": Mary Shelley and the Feminization of Romanticism', *PMLA*, 1980, 95.3, 332-47.

The degree of sympathy or admiration that the text allows for Victor has been much disputed. To what extent can we agree with Walton's assessment of him as a 'glorious spirit' (p. 218) and how much do we see of the benevolence and sweetness he discerns in Victor's face? Earlier critics, such as Robert Kiely in *The Romantic Novel*, lean towards some agreement with Walton. Kiely finds that it is after the disastrous creation, 'by means of the uniqueness and depth of his suffering, that Frankenstein achieves superiority over other men' (p. 158). Victor certainly suffers for his aspirations, and in this respect possibly achieves the status of the Romantic hero (see **Literary background**). The Romantics rather liked to represent themselves as suffering victims; we might recall, for example, Percy Shelley's **melodramatic** line in his 'Ode to the West Wind' (1820): 'I fall upon the thorns of life! I bleed! (line 54). Not surprisingly, they were rather sympathetic towards Milton's Satan in *Paradise Lost*, the archangel who aspires to rival God yet who is 'only supreme / In misery' (IV. 91–2). One might, of course, counter that the monster surely suffers more, and the two characters, Victor and the monster, seem to vie with each other for the right to claim the most suffering. 'Blasted as thou wert,' the monster says over the dead body of Victor, 'my agony was still superior to thine' (p. 223). So who, if anyone, we might ask, truly achieves the status of the suffering Romantic hero?

Like the monster, Victor is an isolated individual; his alienation from society, however, is self-imposed. While the monster longs for the companionship and affection he is denied, Victor rejects the family and friends who love him; he claims this is necessary in order to pursue his quest for the secret of life. There are many suggestions in the text, however, that Victor is rebelling against all human ties, against normal human relationships that bind one to a family and community, against familial and sexual love, against all relationships that might interfere with the pursuit of self-satisfaction (see **Themes**).

So what is the true nature of Victor's crime? Victor is offered to us as the Promethean rebel, the quester after knowledge, and this, in itself, may be admirable. Is his sin to attempt to usurp the role of God in creating life? Is his sin to refuse to take responsibility for what he creates? (see **Analogy and allusion**, on **The myth of Prometheus**).

THE MONSTER

In spite of his unnatural origins, the monster can initially be seen as a new Adam or a **noble savage**. Essentially benevolent, innocent and freed from prejudice, he represents the possibility of a new start. Peter Brooks argues in 'Godlike Science/Unhallowed Arts' that the 'story of his education is a classic study of right natural instinct perverted and turned evil by the social milieu' (p. 215). As his education proceeds, as he moves from nature to culture, the monster learns more and more of the injustices of society. As he learns about emotions and comes to desire love and companionship, he is rejected because of his physical repulsiveness. He masters language, but language fails him; rather than allowing him entry into human society, as he had hoped, it only serves to make him more fully aware of his unique origin and his alien nature. His education is part of what makes him miserable. After he is rejected by the De Lacey family, our sympathies are fully with the monster. It is only when he murders William and thereby also causes the death of Justine that he becomes demonic and our sympathies waver. No longer an Adam, he becomes Satan, the fallen angel (see **Analogy and allusion**).

The monster, understandably considering his reading material, is eloquent, a master of **rhetoric**, and he convinces both the reader and Victor that he should have a companion. He is aware it is his misery in isolation that makes him malicious. He turns on Victor's family and friends because they have what he is denied: the comforts of affection. In so far as he is Victor's **double**, he murders all those whom Victor has already attempted to cut off in his obsessive search for the secret of life. In this respect, he may represent Victor's own

 CHECK THE FILM

Search for a discussion of James Whale's classic 1931 *Frankenstein* at **http://members. aon.at/ frankenstein/**. Does the image of Boris Karloff as the monster conform to your vision of the character? What do you think the addition of the famous scene with the little girl Maria added to the story and why do you think this was subsequently cut?

aggressive instincts, his fears of the family and of women, his horror of normal sexuality (see **Themes**).

CHECK THE FILM
In most film versions of *Frankenstein*, the difficulties of reproducing the narrative form of the novel means that the character of Walton is eliminated. What effect does this have on the story? Roger Corman's 1990 *Frankenstein Unbound*, based on a novel by Brian Aldiss, is a reworking of Shelley's *Frankenstein* that offers a substitute for Walton. The inventor and time traveller Joseph Buchanan, testing his latest laser gun, creates a distortion in the time-space continuum that leads him to be teleported back to Switzerland in 1817 where he meets Frankenstein, the monster, and Mary Shelley. There is a useful discussion of this film at **http://members.aon.at/frankenstein/**.

ROBERT WALTON

In some respects, Walton may be seen as a **double** for Victor Frankenstein. He rebels against his father's dying injunction that he should not go to sea in much the same way as Victor rebels against Alphonse Frankenstein's dismissal of his scientific interests: each son subsequently pursues the forbidden. Like Victor, Walton is obsessed by his quest, and like Victor, he leaves the placid domestic world represented by his sister for the outside world of action and achievement. 'My life might have been passed in ease and luxury,' he notes, 'but I preferred glory to every enticement that wealth placed in my way' (p. 17). Again like Victor, he alternates between offering this selfish explanation of his obsession and a more altruistic justification: 'you cannot contest the inestimable benefit which I shall confer on all mankind to the last generation' (p. 16).

There are also significant differences, however, between the two men. Walton is not quite so alienated an individual as Victor. Rather than rejecting companionship, Walton longs for an intimate friend with whom to share his ideas and dreams. Among his crew, 'unsoftened by cultivation' (p. 20), he finds no one, and this makes the appearance of Victor all the more welcome. Furthermore, in his search for knowledge, Walton is not isolated in the manner of Victor, whose 'midnight labours' and 'secret toil' (p. 54) keep him completely alone. Walton must rely on his crew to help fulfil his ambitions, and when they insist on returning home, force him to fulfil his responsibilities towards them, he is saved from falling into the trap of Victor's rampant individualism.

CAROLINE AND ALPHONSE FRANKENSTEIN

Caroline primarily serves to establish an ideal of femininity. Before her marriage, she has a certain hardiness and independence. Her father's pride makes him willing to remain idle and suffer, and let his daughter suffer, while he waits for employment suited to his position, but when he is ill, Caroline does 'plain work' (p. 32) to support him. Hardiness is nevertheless mixed with the tendency towards self-abnegation which will soon be cultivated. Significantly, it is the image of Caroline 'in an agony of despair, kneeling by the coffin of her dead father' (p. 78) that is immortalised by her husband; this, as Kate Ellis observes in 'Monsters in the Garden', is 'her finest hour' (p. 129). While there is clearly deep love between Caroline and Alphonse, her husband's protective care soon establishes Caroline as a passive dependent. Caroline actively participates in the wider world outside the domestic circle only when she is 'guardian angel to the afflicted' (p. 34). The rest of her time is spent in devoting herself to her family and in **metaphorically** enacting what she later literally performs: in the ultimate act of self-denial, she dies saving Elizabeth. Alphonse Frankenstein, who 'passed his younger days perpetually occupied by the affairs of his country' (p. 31) becomes a husband and father only late in life. He then retires completely from the world, emphasising the **dichotomy** between the public sphere of action and the private sphere of the domestic affections which pervades the novel. Alphonse and Caroline are indulgent parents, but in their desire to preserve domestic tranquillity and to guide their son with a 'silken cord' (p. 34), they perhaps do not allow Victor sufficient independence. His life is 'remarkably secluded and domestic' (p. 45). When he finally leaves this hot-house world of the family, where all are engaged in 'endeavouring to bestow mutual pleasure' (p. 45), and goes to university, Victor reflects how 'I had often, when at home, thought it hard to remain during my youth cooped up in one place, and had longed to enter the world' (p. 45). For the first time, freed from the duties to his family, he can act as an individual (see also **Themes**).

ELIZABETH

A 'garden rose among dark-leaved brambles' (p. 35), Elizabeth is initially singled out for her beauty and this remains one of her most notable characteristics. The Frankenstein family moulds her into the 'ideal' woman, a role she avidly embraces. She is set apart, like the monster, and viewed as a being of a 'distinct species' (p. 34). Religious **imagery** colours all descriptions of the 'heaven-sent' (p. 34) Elizabeth, whose name means 'gift of God'. With her

> **CONTEXT**
>
> The separation of male and female spheres of activity characteristic of the bourgeois family is associated with changes linked to the Industrial Revolution: it occurred once commodity production had been separated from the home; that is, after male and female labour was divided, with female activity regarded as reproductive, giving birth and looking after children, and linked to the home, the private sphere, and male activity associated with commodity production, with the public sphere.

CHECK THE FILM

Kenneth Branagh's 1994 *Mary Shelley's Frankenstein* offers an interesting take on Elizabeth, played by Helena Bonham-Carter. Do you think she is presented here in a more independent manner? What do you think of the addition of her resurrection at the end, and her subsequent suicide? Do the changes made by Branagh conflict with or confirm any of the major motifs of the novel? You may find it interesting to read Michael Eberle-Sinatra's 'Science, Gender and Otherness in Shelley's *Frankenstein* and Kenneth Branagh's Film Adaptation', *European Romantic Review* 9.2 ,1988, 253–70.

'celestial eyes' and 'saintly soul' (p. 38), she is regarded with reverential attachment by all. She is highly spiritualised and, unlike later voluptuous screen Elizabeths, less a creature of flesh and blood than a 'living spirit of love' (p. 38). Elizabeth is also frequently regarded as a possession; 'I have a pretty present for my Victor' (p. 35), Caroline announces, and Victor immediately sees Elizabeth as his to 'protect, love, and cherish' (p. 36). She is generally characterised in terms of her effect on others. Elizabeth's feminine ability to 'soften and attract' (p. 38) seems to be woman's most treasured gift. Self-effacing and passive, she is the complete opposite of the rather egotistical Victor. Her concerns are limited to the domestic circle and she feels rewarded for any 'exertions by seeing none but happy, kind faces' (p. 64). She is totally ineffectual, however, in dealing with the outside world. Her attempts to save Justine are pathetic, inevitable failures: 'I will melt the stony hearts of your enemies by my tears and prayers' (p. 87), she promises, but softening and attracting, tears and prayers, are of little use in the face of the judge's 'harsh unfeeling reason' (p. 89). Frustrated by her own powerlessness, Elizabeth seeks refuge in the typically feminine response: 'I wish,' she cries to Justine, 'that I were to die with you' (p. 88).

SAFIE AND THE DE LACEYS

The description of Safie in the De Lacey household, with its more balanced view of sexual roles, effectively prevents the reader from concluding that Shelley views Elizabeth's position and the role divisions of the Frankensteins as either inevitable or desirable. Safie's successes clearly point out the trouble with transforming women into cherubs. Like Caroline, Safie's mother may be said to be rescued by a man; her rescue, however, more openly involves the exchange of one form of bondage for another, and she rejects both. Instead of resigning herself to a life-long devotion to her deliverer, she cultivates rebellion in her daughter by teaching her to aspire to 'higher powers of intellect and an independence of spirit' (p. 124). Consequently, Safie is less than pleased at the prospect of being 'immured within the walls of a haram, allowed only to occupy herself with infantile amusements' (p. 124). This situation, one might suspect, would hold a certain charm for Elizabeth. While Safie possesses the admired feminine qualities of gentleness and affection, she combines these with the masculine qualities of independence and action. Not content to wait for rescue, she defies parental and social tyranny and makes the trip to Germany on her own initiative.

The members of the De Lacey family are characterised in less detail. They seem to be paragons of virtue: noble, hard-working, pure of heart, affectionate and moral. By showing these splendid qualities to be of little help to them when forced into conflict with more unscrupulous characters, Shelley suggests it will take more than a few virtuous individuals to challenge a powerful and corrupt society. It is also interesting to note that, no matter how good and benevolent these characters may be, they immediately reject the monster when they see him: the prejudice against the alien, against what is physically different and horrific, is, Shelley suggests, pervasive even amongst the most open-minded and charitable of beings.

CLERVAL

Clerval in many ways is the male version of Safie. He is a balanced character, an idealised form of a Romantic poet, and combines masculine ambition and independence with feminine gentleness, affection, and sensitivity. His preference is for the softer landscapes in contrast to Victor, who is linked with the grandeur and isolation of mountain peaks. This contrast, as Peter Dale Scott notes in 'Vital Artifice' (Levine, ed., 1979), is reflected in the naming of the two characters, Clerval suggesting 'clear valley' while Frankenstein may be translated as 'open rock' (p. 194). Clerval prefers the Persian and Arabic tales of fancy and passion to the 'manly and heroical poetry of Greece and Rome' (p. 69) and calls forth 'the better feelings' (p. 70) of Victor's heart.

THEMES

BIRTH AND CREATION

In giving life to his creature, Victor usurps the role of God. Fired by enthusiasm during his first experiments, he imagines how 'A new species would bless me as its creator and source … No father could claim the gratitude of his child so completely as I should deserve

QUESTION

What produces the difference in the characters of Safie and Elizabeth and what role is played by their education?

CHECK THE BOOK

If you are interested in learning more about the harems of the Turkish sultans, Carla Coco's *Secrets of the Harem* ,1997, is a good read and also full of useful information, making careful distinctions between fact and fantasy.

CHECK THE NET

A hypertext version of Peake's *Presumption; or, The Fate of Frankenstein* is available at **http://www.rc. umd.edu/editions/ contemps/peake/**.

CHECK THE FILM

Kenneth Branagh, in his 1994 *Mary Shelley's Frankenstein*, emphasises the idea of birth with the creature being put in a tank full of amniotic fluid. Do you think this scene is true to the spirit of the original novel?

theirs' (p. 54). In her 1831 Introduction, Mary Shelley suggests that this is his main crime: his presumption in displacing God as creator. When the story was adapted for the stage in 1823, it was, in fact, given the title *Presumption; or, The Fate of Frankenstein*. Nevertheless, the world Shelley creates is entirely secular: Christian myth serves only to provide **analogies**. Perhaps we need to consider whether there is in fact any suggestion within the text that Victor should not have attempted the act of creation. Perhaps the crime upon which Shelley focuses is not what he does, but what he fails to do: nurture his creation. Victor's ambition and achievement may well be heroic; chaos only ensues because he is incapable of bearing responsibility for what he produces. On the other hand, Victor's description of his 'secret toil' (p. 54) does suggest he is engaged in something shameful or unlawful.

Frankenstein also seeks to usurp the power of women, and in this he may be revealing his rebellion against the normal family unit and the responsibilities involved in belonging to such a unit. He may also be revealing a fear of the natural processes of birth, possibly echoing Shelley's own **ambivalence** about childbirth. First pregnant at sixteen, and almost constantly pregnant during the next five years, Shelley lost most of her children soon after they were born. Victor's 'workshop of filthy creation' (p. 55) may have womb-like **connotations**. Furthermore, as Ellen Moers implies in 'Female Gothic' (Levine, ed., 1979), the description of the newly created monster may suggest the appearance of the newborn baby.

ALIENATION

The sufferings of both Victor and the monster are primarily caused by their alienation from others. The monster's isolation is imposed upon him by others: the creator who abandons him and the people who shun him. He longs for companionship and affection and his unhappiness and subsequent violence result from his awareness that he will never experience the love he sees around him. 'I am malicious because I am miserable' (p. 145), he tells Victor, and asks for a female companion to make him happy again. Victor, however, is horrified by the nearly completed female form and the thought of the monster's family life; he tears the female to pieces. When the monster murders Elizabeth, he is only doing what Victor has already done to him. Victor repeatedly insists that his isolation is also imposed because of the monster's crimes: he must be an outcast. Nevertheless, he actually chooses to isolate himself from family and friends in order to carry out his scientific experiments. We need to consider further the nature of what he rejects in order better to understand this self-imposed isolation.

THE FAMILY AND THE DOMESTIC AFFECTIONS

Percy Shelley's Preface claims that the chief concern of the novel is 'the exhibition of the amiableness of domestic affection, and the excellence of universal virtue' (p. 14) and domesticity is indeed frequently idealised. It is the domestic affections for which the creature longs and that Victor repeatedly holds up as the ideal to which he should have aspired. The home is represented as a paradise or temple, the woman as the presiding angel. Nevertheless, as Kate Ellis has most convincingly argued in 'Monsters in the Garden: Mary Shelley and the Bourgeois Family' (Levine, ed., 1979), it is quite possible to read the novel as questioning the value of the domestic affections and as an attack on, rather than a celebration of, the institution of the family. Strictly enforced artificial role distinctions, Shelley demonstrates, result in the creation of a passive, dependent woman who ultimately becomes the monster who must be rejected, and like the creature, no longer the slave but the master. Victor certainly needs to escape the suffocating 'silken cord' (p. 34) of the home in order to fulfil his desires; there is no room for ambition or individualism in the domestic world. The treatment of the creature by the De Lacey household points to another defect in the domestic world: its insularity. Ideal though this family may be, it functions only by excluding anything that appears as a threat to its security. The creature devotes himself to the destruction of ideal domesticity once he recognises he is doomed to be excluded from it, and in this he may be acting as Victor's **double**

THE DOUBLE

The popular tendency to refer to the creature as Frankenstein is appropriate considering Shelley's use of the motif of the **double**, a frequent motif in much Gothic fiction.

 CHECK THE BOOK

A discussion of the domestic affections in other works by Shelley can be found in Kate Ferguson Ellis, 'Subversive Surfaces: The Limits of Domestic Affection', in *The Other Mary Shelley: Beyond Frankenstein*, eds Audrey Fisch, Anne K. Mellor, and Esther H. Schor, 1993, pp. 220–34.

CONTEXT

Shelley also exploits the motif the double in some of her short stories: 'Transformation', 1831, is a Gothic fairy tale that focuses upon a deformed Satanic dwarf who exchanges identities with a vindictive and dissolute youth, and 'The Mourner',1830, considers monstrosity, the double, and family relationships.

CHECK THE BOOK

The male fear of female sexuality is one of the issues addressed by Anne Mellor in *Mary Shelley: Her Life, Her Fiction and Her Monsters*, 1988.

When he refers to the creature as 'my own spirit let loose from the grave ... forced to destroy all that was dear to me' (p. 77), Victor provides the clearest expression of the notion that he and the monster may be doubles, with the monster acting out Victor's own aggressions. In creating the monster, the civilised being lets loose the violent, monstrous self contained within, full of primitive emotions, and this monstrous force can be seen as acting out the repressed desires of the civilised being. Doubling extends even further, however: Walton can be seen as another Frankenstein, for example, and it has even been argued that Elizabeth and the creature can be seen as one.

THE FEAR OF SEXUALITY

In creating the monster and usurping the role of woman, Victor is also rejecting normal human sexuality. His terrible nightmare after the creation of the monster seems to support the idea that Victor is repelled by normal sexuality. When he attempts to kiss Elizabeth, she turns into a corpse, the corpse of Victor's mother, perhaps indicating also that Victor is frightened by incestuous desires (see **Detailed commentaries: Text 1**). His response to his father's suggestion that he marry may be read as a highly telling revelation of his feelings about sexuality: 'Alas! to me the idea of an immediate union with my Elizabeth was one of horror and dismay' (p. 151). He explains that this is because the threat of the monster still hangs over him, but other readings are certainly possible. The same may be said of his words to Elizabeth on their wedding night: 'Oh! peace, peace, my love,' he tells her, 'this night, and all will be safe: but this night is dreadful, very dreadful' (p. 194) possibly manages to misinterpret the monster's threat: 'I shall be with you on your wedding-night' (p. 168). Since it is uttered soon after Victor destroys the female companion, to the reader it seems quite clear that the threat is to Elizabeth, and yet Victor interprets it as a threat against him, and he leaves Elizabeth, on the pretext of saving her from the sight of the combat he expects, alone in the bedroom to be murdered by the monster. Here the notion of the **double** again aids in interpretation. It is possible to see the monster as an externalisation of Victor's sexual impulses, the ugliness of the monster suggesting his horror of normal sexuality. The monster assures Victor that he will be with him on his wedding night, the time when Victor can no longer avoid confronting his own sexuality. He leaves Elizabeth alone, but that part of himself he rejects, his sexuality, does not disappear. Instead, it turns destructive; he unleashes upon her this ugly violent thing: the embodiment of his twisted sexual impulses.

THE CRITIQUE OF SOCIETY

While the family is the institution most thoroughly examined and analysed, throughout *Frankenstein* there is a more general challenge to and criticism of the established social order and its institutions. In the story of the De Laceys, in the treatment of the creature, and in the trial of Justine, human injustice is repeatedly emphasised. As Elizabeth observes after the execution of Justine, 'men appear to me as monsters thirsting for each other's blood' (p. 92). She may immediately retract her words, saying 'Yet I am certainly unjust' (p. 92), but the idea that society itself is monstrous is one of the key themes of the novel. Social institutions such as the law and the Church are repeatedly shown to be corrupt. Shelley frequently uses the monster as her mouthpiece in her critique of oppression and inequality in society. From his own experiences and those of the De Lacey family, the monster learns much about social injustice, and provides some pointed economic critiques. He sees how 'high and unsullied descent united with riches' (p. 120) are the possessions esteemed above all, and that without at least one of these, a man would be considered 'a vagabond and a slave, doomed to waste his powers for the profit of the chosen few' (p. 120).

THE MONSTROUS AND THE HUMAN

As a rational and eloquent being, Victor's creation blurs distinctions between the human and the non-human. To call him, in what has become the accepted manner, the 'monster' is problematic; we need to recognise that in so doing we may in part be assuming the perspective of Victor Frankenstein and all the other characters who reject him in horror simply on the basis of his frightening appearance. While the term monster is often used to describe anything horrifyingly unnatural or excessively large, it initially had far more precise connotations, and these are of some significance for the ways in which the monstrous comes to function within the Gothic. Etymologically speaking, the monster is something to be

CHECK THE FILM
Ridley Scott's 1982 *Bladerunner,* one of the best films ever made about artificial humans, has many interesting connections to *Frankenstein.* Particularly notable is the relationship of the replicants to human society. Do you think that this film problematises the nature of the monstrous and the human in a similar way to Shelley's novel?

The monstrous and the human continued

shown, something that serves to demonstrate (Latin, *monstrare*: to demonstrate) and to warn (Latin, *monere*: to warn). From classical times through the Renaissance, monsters were interpreted either as signs of divine anger or portents of impending disasters. These early monsters are frequently constructed out of ill-assorted parts, like the Griffin, with the head and wings of an eagle combined with the body and paws of a lion. Alternately, they are incomplete, lacking essential parts, or, like the mythological Hydra with its many heads, grotesquely excessive. By the eighteenth century the horrific appearance of the monster had begun to serve an increasingly moral function. As Alexander Pope writes in his *Essay on Man* (1733–4), 'Vice is a monster of so frightful mien / As, to be hated, needs but to be seen' (lines 217–8). By providing a visible warning of the results of vice and folly, monsters promote virtuous behaviour.

> ### CONTEXT
>
> Monsters do cultural work in that they define and construct the politics of the normal, pointing to those boundaries that must not be crossed. They may however, through difference also challenge definitions of the normal and disrupt systems of classification. How does monstrosity function in *Frankenstein*?

Through difference, whether in appearance or behaviour, monsters function to define and construct the politics of the 'normal'. Located at the margins of culture, they police the boundaries of the human, pointing to those lines that must not be crossed. In most Gothic fiction of the eighteenth and nineteenth centuries, the monster is admitted to the text only to be ultimately expelled or repudiated. Limits and boundaries are reinstated as the monster is dispatched, good is distinguished from evil and self from other. Shelley's novel, however, problematises the very notions of monstrosity and humanity. If the creature's appearance is a visible warning, it is a warning of Victor's folly, not his own. And although the creature's exterior may be horrific, he is, at least initially, certainly not 'frighteningly unnatural'; rather, he is far more natural and humane than the 'father' who rejects him, the villagers who stone him, the ungrateful father who shoots him. It is only when he is exposed to, and suffers from, the viciousness of human society that he himself begins to demonstrate violent behaviour, to act as the monster his appearance suggests him to be. Can we say that real monsters are created by suffering and oppression? Then again, from what we have seen of his treatment at the hands of ordinary humans up until this point, we might also say that this new 'monstrous' behaviour is quite generally characteristic of the 'human', and not just displayed by the oppressed. It is significant that it is the decision of society's leaders to execute Justine that causes Elizabeth to declare how, in their violence and cruelty, people appear to be 'monsters thirsting for each other's blood'. What, Shelley forces us to ask, is a monster? How do we define the monstrous, and how the human? Can we even make a clear distinction between the two?

TECHNIQUES

NARRATIVE TECHNIQUES

The complex structure of *Frankenstein* involves **framed** or **embedded narratives**, what has been called a Chinese box structure of stories within stories. In the outermost frame narrative of four letters, Walton writes to his sister Mrs Saville. At this stage, we have an **epistolary** narrative. This is dropped however as we move to an embedded narrative: Victor's account of his life, Chapters 1–10. Victor's narrative then serves in turn to frame the creature's embedded narrative, Chapters 11–16, where he recounts his tale, and that of the De Lacey family, to Victor, who in turn recounts it to Walton. The narrative then returns to Frankenstein until Chapter 24, when Walton again takes over, and we return to the frame narrative for the conclusion of the story. The anarchic energy of the text is formally restrained by this tight structure, and in this sense may be profitably compared with Emily Brontë's *Wuthering Heights*, another nineteenth-century novel with a similarly complicated and tight narrative structure enclosing the anarchic rebellions of the characters against the established order.

QUESTION

Discuss *Frankenstein*'s shifts in narrative perspective. What is the function of presenting three different narrative positions?

The problem with using the Chinese box analogy to describe the narrative structure of *Frankenstein* is that this term tends to suggest that each story is entirely separate, complete in itself. The **narratives** are not **linear** or complete however; we are not taken directly from the beginning of one **narrator's** tale to the end and then move to the next narrator's tale. To give an example, Walton's initial narrative provides us with an account of Victor's predicament that would, in a linear narrative, come near the end of Victor's narration. The narratives, rather than being complete and whole in themselves, are interrelated and interdependent.

CHECK THE BOOK

For a discussion of *Frankenstein's* narratives, see Beth Newman, 'Narratives of Seduction and the Seductions of Narrative: The Frame Structure of *Frankenstein*' in Fred Botting, ed., *Frankenstein*. New Casebooks, 1995.

The convention of frame narratives is that we accept that the stories contained within the frame narrative are remembered and transcribed virtually word for word by the frame narrator. We might, then, ask to what degree differences in voice are effaced by this process, if voice is considered in its admittedly rather vague sense of the distinctive features of tone and style. Is the voice in the monster's narrative all that distinct from that in Walton's or Victor's? Are there discernible differences which help to express unique personalities, or are the markers which would allow us to distinguish between narrators effaced by the frame narrator's recounting of the other stories? Some critics have suggested that, since all the narratives ultimately come to us from the frame narrator, distinctions between voices are blurred and the question basic to most narrative theories, who is speaking, becomes problematised. *Frankenstein* is written in the **first-person narrative**, but do we have one or three first-person narrators?

The structure also draws attention to the presence of a listener or **narratee** for each narrator, encouraging the reader to consider what purpose each narrator has in speaking, what influence he is attempting to exert over the narratee. Their stories, at least in the case of Victor and the monster, are clearly told in a way designed to achieve a specific effect. The monster's narrative is an attempt to persuade Victor to assume his responsibilities towards his creation and to construct a mate for him. What strategies does the monster use? How does he emphasise his point about the need for companionship and love? Victor similarly has specific aims in telling his tale to Walton; he may begin by claiming to use his fate as a warning to Walton, but by the time his narrative concludes, his real purpose has become clear. As the monster uses his eloquence to make him promise him a mate, so Victor attempts, but fails, to make Walton promise to take over his quest to destroy the monster.

We might also consider how reliable the narrators are, both in their assessment of themselves and in their interpretation of other characters and situations. When Victor compares his feelings to those of Justine, condemned to be executed, and assures us that the **'tortures of the accused did not equal mine'** (p. 85), do we perhaps feel that he is a little too self-absorbed to be the best interpreter of other people's feelings? Does Victor even really understand his own fears? He tells us he does not want to rush into marriage with Elizabeth because he first has to deal with the problem of the monster, but his dreams suggest there is more to it than this, that he would rather dabble with test tubes than procreate in the normal way.

The narrative style additionally serves to invite us to look for echoes and **parallels** which link the stories together and simultaneously to identify differences between the three characters. Walton's ambitions, for example, make him a potential Frankenstein, and he too is isolated and alienated from the domestic world. However, Walton truly seems to long for the affection and companionship that Victor spurns, and in this sense he is more closely linked to the monster. In addition, no matter how alienated Walton may feel in the icy wastes of the Arctic, he has his crew, a community of sorts who prevent him from indulging in the kind of rampant individualism that destroys Victor.

Finally, we need to consider whether there is **closure** or if the novel remains open-ended. As it is so difficult to fix one meaning or message to Shelley's *Frankenstein*, then on the level of interpretation there is no closure. Although we seem to come to a decisive end with the death of Victor and Walton's decision to return home, there is actually no real closure on the level of plot either. The monster vows to immolate himself. As Fred Botting points out in *Making Monstrous*, 1991, however, 'from the textual evidence the reader can never know what happens to the monster' (p. 43) This ending is, for us, for ever deferred, something projected in the future, and Shelley leaves the reader, like the monster, '**lost in darkness and distance**' (p. 223).

ANALOGY AND ALLUSION

Frankenstein is full of both **analogies** drawn between the characters and other figures from literature and myth and **allusions** to various other texts; indeed, it could be said that, as the monster is constructed out of fragments of corpses, the text is constructed out of fragments of other texts. The major stories which Shelley appropriates and reworks are the myth of Prometheus, Milton's *Paradise Lost*, and, to a lesser degree, Coleridge's *The Rime of the Ancient Mariner*.

 CHECK THE NET
Search for 'Prometheus' to learn more about the various versions of this myth. One useful site with images is **http://www.pathguy.com/promethe.htm**.

The myth of Prometheus

The full title of Shelley's novel, *Frankenstein or The Modern Prometheus*, invites us to make an analogy between Victor Frankenstein and the mythic Prometheus. There are two variations of the Prometheus myth. In Ovid, Prometheus is a creator who moulds the first human out of clay. In Aeschylus, he steals fire from the heavens and gives it to humans; he is subsequently punished by the gods for his presumption with eternal torment: he is chained to Mount Caucasus, where an eagle preys on his liver all day, that liver then being renewed every night. These two myths gradually converged, and the fire became the vital principle with which Prometheus animated his clay images.

If we consider Victor as a reworking of this mythic Prometheus, the implication is that he is one of those admirable overreachers who refuse to accept limitations and are punished. He becomes the embodiment of an unquenchable thirst for knowledge, a rebel against limitations set by the gods, an admirable man who is punished for his daring. However, when we consider the actual characterisation of Victor, problems immediately appear. First, we have to ask how admirable Victor really is: do we accept Walton's assessment of him as the divine wanderer who possesses qualities which elevate him far above any normal man. Is he really driven by a desire to help mankind or is he driven by a simple desire for personal glory? Then, we also need to consider whether the main sin for which Victor is punished is the daring act of creation, as it was with Prometheus, or if it is his failure to take responsibility for and nurture the creature he produces. Does his crime lie in what he does, or in what he fails to do? We might also ask in what sense he is a 'modern' Prometheus. One answer might be that Shelley links the myth with current scientific theories, suggesting that the spark of life is not fire but electricity. Alternatively, he may be a 'modern' Prometheus because this is such a secular world; there is no divine machinery here, no god against whom to rebel.

Another answer could be that Shelley is providing an implicit criticism of Romanticism (see **Literary background**). Prometheus was a popular figure with the Romantic poets, who emphasised his role as the suffering champion of mankind, and saw in him the

CONTEXT

Aeschylus (525–456 BC) is the earliest Greek tragic poet whose work survives. One of the surviving plays is *Prometheus Bound*, possibly part of a trilogy that began with *Prometheus the Fire Carrier* and ended with *Prometheus Unbound*.

archetypal rebel hero. In *Prometheus Unbound* (published in 1820), a reworking of Aeschylus's tragedies, Percy Shelley presents him as 'the type of the highest perfection of moral and intellectual nature, impelled by the purest and the truest motives to the best and noblest ends' (*Poetical Works*, p. 205). He also becomes, as creator, the embodiment of the Romantic poet, the isolated heroic artist fearless in his quest to bring light to men, punished by the authority against whom he rebels, but still noble in his suffering. Contemporary critics often consider that Mary's modern Prometheus provides a criticism of the egocentric and antisocial tendencies of Romanticism, suggesting there is little hope for humanity in such self-absorption. In this reading, Shelley is seen to push the Romantic figure of the isolated creative imagination to its extremes and clearly demonstrates the dangers associated with solitude and introversion.

Adam and Paradise Lost

> Did I request thee, Maker, from my clay
> To mould Me man? Did I solicit thee
> From darkness to promote me?– (*Paradise Lost*, X.743–5)

Shelley chooses for her **epigraph** a quotation from *Paradise Lost*, one of the books in the monster's library, and this, along with the many other references to Milton's epic poem throughout the novel, suggest that we need always to keep this story in mind when reading *Frankenstein*. The epigraph immediately encourages us to associate Victor with God and the monster with Adam, and this seems appropriate since, as creator, Victor assumes the role of God, and the 'man' he creates is the monster. The analogy, however, is problematic. If Victor is associated with God, how can he also be the Promethean rebel against God? Furthermore, while the monster certainly fits the role of Adam, he becomes also the demon, assuming the role of Satan, the fallen archangel who engineers the fall of Adam and brings Sin and Death into the world. When the monster confronts Victor, after the murder of William, he declares that he has been changed by his exclusion from paradise: 'I am thy creature; I ought to be thy Adam; but I am rather the fallen angel, whom thou drivest from joy for no misdeed' (p. 100). The monster even echoes Satan's words in *Paradise Lost* when he declares to

CONTEXT

John Milton's *Paradise Lost* tells the story of the creation of Adam and Eve and how they came to lose their place in Eden. More importantly for the Romantics, it also tells the story of Lucifer, an angel in heaven who led his followers in a war against God and was consequently exiled from heaven; his desire for revenge leads him to plan the downfall of mankind. A useful web site on *Paradise Lost* can be found at **http://www.paradise lost.org/**.

Walton that, after his potential companion had been destroyed, 'Evil thenceforth became my good' (p. 220).

An additional complication arises when we see the monster as Victor's **double** (see **Themes**). If the monster is satanic, Victor, by association, can then be linked not only with Prometheus and with God, but also with Satan, the fallen angel. While the analogy drawn between the monster and Satan focuses our attention on the creature's horrific acts of savage violence, the analogy drawn between Victor and Satan focuses our attention more on Victor's pride and ambition. In attempting to displace God, he demonstrates the same pride as Satan, who had similar aspirations. Commenting upon his torment of guilt, Victor draws upon the following **simile**: 'Like the archangel who aspired to omnipotence, I am chained in an eternal hell' (p. 211). Victor's hell is within him, it is hell as a psychological state, but this is also true of the hell so powerfully described by Satan in *Paradise Lost*. The analogy drawn between Victor and Satan is not necessarily entirely negative; Milton's Satan is an interesting, even glamorous figure, nothing like the shadowy figure of the Bible. Percy Shelley even considered that Satan was morally superior to God in Milton's poem, and many of the Romantic poets admired the grandeur and boldness of his aspirations. While Victor must be condemned for the neglect of his creature, it is possible that he too can still be admired for his bold aspirations, his refusal to be satisfied with a mundane and uneventful existence with his family, and his attempt to give mankind a power thought to belong to God alone. To come to that conclusion, however, perhaps we need to be convinced that his work is driven by the desire to benefit others and not by more selfish motives.

The Rime of the Ancient Mariner

Coleridge's poem was first published in 1798 in *Lyrical Ballads*. The story concerns an ancient mariner who meets three men on their way to a wedding feast; he detains one and, with his 'glittering eye', holds him while he recounts his story. He tells how his ship was drawn towards the South Pole by a storm and the ship became surrounded by ice. In this world devoid of living things an albatross flies through the fog and the crew greets it with joy. It seems to be a

CONTEXT

In turning Satan into the hero of *Paradise Lost*, the Romantic poets suggest their rebellion against authoritative structures. If you are familiar with any of the male Romantics' representations of Satanic hero-villains, you might want to consider how Mary Shelley's use of the figure is different.

CHECK THE BOOK

For further information on the Romantic attitude to Satan, see Kenneth Gross's 'Satan and the Romantic Satan' in *Re-Membering Milton: Essays on the Texts and Traditions*, eds Margaret Ferguson and Mary Nyquist, 1987.

good omen. The ice splits, the ship begins to move, and the bird flies along with it. Inexplicably, the mariner shoots it, and for this act of cruelty a curse descends upon the ship. She is driven towards the Equator and becalmed on a silent rotting sea under the burning sun. The dead bird is hung around the neck of the mariner. Death and Life-in-Death appear, playing dice on a skeleton ship. When it vanishes all the crew die with the exception of the mariner; he is left alone in an alien world. Moved by the beauty of watersnakes in the moonlight, the mariner blesses them, and the albatross falls from his neck. He is saved, but, in penance, condemned to travel the world teaching love and reverence for all God's creatures.

The most obvious connection with the story of the ancient mariner is Walton's journey into the frozen wastes of the Arctic; Walton even quotes the poem when the ship is trapped in the ice. However, the mariner's story actually seems to throw more light upon the experiences of the other characters. Like Victor, the Ancient Mariner defies God. In shooting the albatross he disturbs the natural order and his world, like Victor's, is transformed into a nightmare vision of an alien universe, a meaningless and terrifying wasteland, a world without God. Even after the mariner is forgiven, we are left with the suspicion that this vision of the world may have been prompted by the mariner's insight into the truth of the human condition. The monster's experiences may offer a similar insight into a godless world, an irrational, terrifying world managed only by human institutions which are corrupt and individuals who are irresponsible and cruel. Furthermore, like both Victor and the monster, the mariner is an alienated individual. Once he shoots the albatross, he is no longer at peace with himself, and he is shunned by the wider community. Even after he is forgiven, although he becomes aware of the joys of family and community life, he is forced to do penance which keeps him still a solitary, marginal figure, eternally wandering the world. The poem offers a haunting portrayal of the guilt and loneliness that Shelley also captures through the experiences of her characters.

LANGUAGE

In the story of *Frankenstein* there is always more emphasis on description than on dramatic action, more emphasis on telling than

CHECK THE NET
There are numerous etexts of Coleridge's 'Rime of the Ancient Mariner' on the net; search 'Coleridge Mariner etext'. For the revised 1817 version with full marginal notes, see **http:// www.bartleby. com/101/549.html**.

CHECK THE NET
Search for a hypertext essay on Coleridge's 'Mariner' by David Miall.

showing. The language is often highly emotional, **melodramatic**, threatening, some critics would say, to fall into absurdity. The creature's language is highly **rhetorical**, but so is much of the book. Indeed, we might ask how much difference we find in the language of the three characters (see **Narrative techniques**). This emphasis on description, however, does not involve a detailed analysis of inner feeling. 'Everything internal,' George Levine claims in *The Endurance of Frankenstein*, 1979, 'is transformed into large public gesture or high rhetorical argument' (p. 19). Alternatively, it remains unexplored, to emerge only indirectly through images or dreams.

QUESTION

Shelley's monster is highly articulate. Why do you think film versions of the story tend to represent him as mute or, at the very least, inarticulate?

It is the monster's eloquence that has received the most attention. We might expect a grunting animal, but what we are confronted with, as Peter Brooks notes in 'Godlike Science/Unhallowed Arts,' is a 'supreme rhetorician of his own situation'; he controls the **antitheses** and **oxymorons** 'that express the pathos of his existence' (p. 206–7). Consider, for example, the impressive use of balance and opposition in his injunction to Victor: 'Remember, that I am thy creature; I ought to be thy Adam; but I am rather the fallen angel, whom thou drivest from joy for no misdeed. Every where I see bliss, from which I alone am irrevocably excluded. I was benevolent and good; misery made me a fiend. Make me happy, and I shall again be virtuous' (p. 100). Victor is indeed eventually persuaded to make him a mate. Language seems to have power in this novel.

Nevertheless, language simultaneously seems inadequate and weak. Characters repeatedly assert their inability to express their feelings in language. Victor, for example, is constantly falling back on such phrases as 'no-one can conceive' or 'I cannot describe' (e.g. pages 54, 85, 92 and 176) While this is a traditional feature of the **Gothic**, it is also a comment upon the inadequacy of language to capture and account for inner experience. This experience, in *Frankenstein*, is more precisely captured **symbolically** in dreams; the nightmare Victor experiences after bringing the monster to life, for example, when Elizabeth is transformed into the corpse of his dead mother, tells us post-Freudian readers all we need to know about Victor's true feelings for his mother and for Elizabeth, and all we need to know about his attitude towards human sexuality (see **Detailed commentaries: Text 1**).

It could be said that *Frankenstein* is all about language: its potential power and the breakdown of that power when faced with the prejudices and insensitivity of a society that tends to privilege the specular, to judge above all on appearances. The first key stage of the monster's education is his recognition of the importance of language. In the hovel adjoining the De Lacey cottage, he sees that people communicate 'their experience and feelings to one another by articulate sounds', and, even more importantly, that the words they speak 'produced pleasure or pain, smiles or sadness' (p. 112); they produce, that is, emotional effects. While aware that his physical appearance would cause only revulsion if he confronted the family, the monster believes that by becoming an adept in the 'godlike science' (p. 112) of language, he will be able through his gentle words to win their affection. His subsequent success with the blind father initially bears out his faith in language, but as soon as the others enter, the importance of appearances reasserts itself, and prejudice against what looks alien and other wins out. The monster has a similar experience in his attempt to persuade Victor to create a mate for him; once again, this is an attempt to gain love and companionship through language. Victor is indeed convinced by his eloquence: 'His words had a strange effect on me. I compassioned him' (p. 147). But the effect is fleeting; as soon as he looks upon the monster, he is again filled with horror for the 'filthy mass that moved and talked' (p. 147). When he next catches sight of this 'filthy mass' at the window of the hut where he is making the female, enough time has passed for the effects of eloquence to have worn off completely. Victor reads in the monster's countenance only malice and treachery, and he tears the female to pieces.

Victor too is noted for his fluency with words, his ability to manipulate language, his 'unparalleled eloquence' (p. 27). His voice, like the Ancient Mariner's glittering eye, compels the listener to attend. When he speaks, Walton notes, the sailors no longer want to return home, no longer despair; they are roused to action, filled with courage. But this does not last; the effect persists only as long as the voice is heard, and once Victor is dead, the sailors insist on Walton turning back. Victor's eloquence also impresses Walton, but, notably, this eloquence fails to persuade him to take over the quest to destroy the monster.

> **CONTEXT**
>
> Another work of Gothic fiction that emerged out of the gathering at the Villa Diodati in the summer of 1816 is John Polidori's *The Vampyre*, 1819; the aristocratic villain, Lord Ruthven, was to establish the type of literary vampire that would predominate for at least a century.

CHECK THE FILM

Jim Sharman's cult film *The Rocky Horror Show,* 1974, is clearly indebted in many ways to Shelley's *Frankenstein*. Does the relationship between Baron Frank'n'furter and his artificial creation Rocky have any connection to the relationship between Frankenstein and his monster?

Insisting on the power of the heard voice, Shelley draws our attention to the difference between reading and hearing narratives; we can only be told of the modulations in the voice of the speaker. It is difficult to convey, through writing, the sound of Victor's 'full-toned voice' (p. 31) whose 'varied intonations', according to Walton, are 'soul-subduing music' (p. 29). We are told the monster's voice is harsh, but we cannot hear that harshness as we read. **Voice** is inevitably a rather vague and not particularly useful technical term in literary studies, and distinctions between narrative voice (as opposed to **narrative point of view**) tend to be distinctions between different ways of addressing the reader; it is, clearly, far easier to determine that a voice is **ironic** or intimate than it is to determine than it is 'full-toned' or harsh.

PART FOUR

CRITICAL HISTORY

ORIGINAL RECEPTION

When *Frankenstein* was first published anonymously in 1818, it was extensively reviewed by many of the important journals of the time. These reviews are notable for three main points. First, most critics simply assumed the author to be a man. The eventual discovery that it was Mary Shelley caused some consternation: the blasphemous ideas expressed were considered particularly unseemly for a woman. Secondly, the style of the novel was generally praised; most agreed with *Blackwood's* (March 1818) assessment of 'the author's original genius and happy power of expression'. Finally, while being impressed by the power and vigour of the work, many reviewers criticised the subject matter and the author's refusal to moralise about Frankenstein's blasphemous act. *The Quarterly Review* of January 1818 provides a typical complaint. After summarising the plot and declaring it to be a 'tissue of horrible and disgusting absurdity', the reviewer concludes: 'Our taste and our judgement alike revolt at this kind of writing, and the greater the ability with which it may be executed the worse it is – it inculcates no lesson of conduct, manners, or morality.'

> **CONTEXT**
>
> In the nineteenth century, blasphemy – treating sacred things with irreverence or disregard – was considered to be a serious crime.

A MINOR WORK

For much of the twentieth century, *Frankenstein* has been considered an interesting novel but by no means 'great literature'. In *Mary Shelley: A Biography*, R. Glynn Grylls, writing in 1938, considered it to be 'a "period piece," of not very good date; historically interesting, but not one of the living novels of the world' (p. 320). It was generally agreed to be a minor work, certainly no masterpiece, relegated to the margins of 'popular' literature and granted even this status only because of Mary Shelley's impressive literary relations. *Frankenstein* was considered of some importance primarily because, the general consensus was, it encapsulated in a conveniently simple form the preoccupations of Romanticism.

Feminist Romantic scholars helped move *Frankenstein* into the spotlight by examining the relationships between the author and her circle. Thematically, the focus was usually on her representations of motherhood and childbirth. Such criticism tended to focus heavily on Shelley's personal life and attempted to read this into her fiction. Ellen Moers, for example, offered an influential 1974 reading of the text as a 'woman's mythmaking on the subject of birth' (reprinted in Levine, 1979, p.2); This rather outdated kind of psycho-biographical criticism sometimes tends to reduce the text to a 'monstrous' symptom of a disturbed psyche.

As the concept of a 'canon' of great works disappeared and the boundaries of 'literature' expanded, *Frankenstein* gradually began to attract more critical attention. In 1979 George Levine and U.C. Knoepflmacher edited a collection of essays, *The Endurance of Frankenstein*, that marked a turning point in *Frankenstein* criticism. While still convinced that *Frankenstein* was 'a "minor" novel, radically flawed by its sensationalism, by the inflexibly public and oratorical nature of even its most intimate passages', Levine argued that *Frankenstein* was the 'most important minor novel in English' (p. 3).

It had become a **metaphor** for our own most crucial cultural concerns, expressing the 'central dualities and tensions of our time by positing a world without God' (p. 8). Approaching the novel from a variety of critical perspectives, feminist, materialist, and psychoanalytical, the essays in this collection clearly demonstrated there was far more to *Frankenstein* than a quaint perspective on Romanticism. Mary Shelley was no longer considered to be simply echoing the ideas of her more illustrious Romantic friends and relations. Instead she was seen as a woman writer offering a female perspective on such issues as birth and the family, and a female critique, rather than a celebration, of the masculine preoccupations of Romanticism.

 CHECK THE NET
To keep up to date in recent publications dealing with Shelley and other nineteenth-century writers, go to the web site New Books in Nineteenth-Century Studies: **http://www.usc.edu/dept/LAS/english/19c/newbooks.html**.

THE LAST TWENTY YEARS

The last twenty years have seen a significant reassessment of *Frankenstein*. Feminist criticism has been of particular importance in this process, stressing the need to consider Shelley as a woman writer who explores women's experience. Materialist and new historical readings have also added new dimensions to a reading of *Frankenstein*, stressing the significance of particular social and economic conditions to our interpretation of the text. By looking at various rewritings and reworkings of the *Frankenstein* myth, from films to cereal boxes to electricity advertisements, critics have also examined the ever changing significance of the monster, the changing cultural anxieties which he is adapted to embody. Psycho-analytical studies, such as William Veeder's *Mary Shelley and Frankenstein* (1986), now complement Freudian readings with Lacanian analysis.

For many of the most recent critics, the text itself is 'monstrous', calling into question traditional values and comfortable categories. The idea of 'monstrosity' itself forms a key issue in Fred Botting's 1991 *Making Monstrous: Frankenstein, Criticism, Theory*, which engages with both the text of *Frankenstein* and the criticism that has attempted to identify and fix the text's significance.

Monstrosity is also a question with which a number of other critics engage in the essays Botting edited for the 1995 Macmillan New Casebook on *Frankenstein*. The question of whether *Frankenstein* is a 'minor' novel is no longer of any concern; as Botting notes in his introduction, literature has 'lost many of its former associations with timeless and ultimate value' (p. 1), and the publication of such a collection of essays as this testifies to the changes that have occurred in the study of literature, 'marking a shift of focus in which literary and popular fiction is studied in relation to a net-work of other writings from political, historical, and cultural spheres' (p. 1).

This collection brings together the most influential readings of the past twenty years and is a useful way for students to familiarise themselves with the various contemporary critical approaches to the novel. For those interested in the ways in which changing social conditions interact with texts, Paul O'Flynn offers a Marxist reading that suggests how the political and economic unrest of the time shapes the social meanings of Shelley's *Frankenstein*, and then considers how different political conditions affect the 1931

CHECK THE BOOK

A useful source of information on the literary and cultural contexts of *Frankenstein* and its reception history is Tim Morton, *A Routledge Literary Sourcebook on Mary Shelley's Frankenstein*, 2002.

QUESTION

Elizabeth Gaskell famously described Frankenstein's creation as a 'monster of many human qualities, ungifted with a soul'. Using this as your starting point – you don't have to agree – explore the role of the monster in Shelley's novel.

CHECK THE BOOK

Johanna Smith's *Mary Shelley: Frankenstein*, 2000, presents the 1831 text of Mary Shelley's novel along with critical essays from contemporary psychoanalytic, Marxist, feminist and cultural studies perspectives. An additional essay demonstrates how various critical perspectives can be combined.

Universal film of *Frankenstein*, with Karloff as the monster, and the British Hammer films, *The Curse of Frankenstein* and its sequels, produced in the 1950s and 1960s. Chris Baldick traces the political meanings of the word 'monster'; Margaret Homans offers a feminist read-ing using psychoanalysis to address the absence of the maternal; Beth Newman provides a deconstructive reading of the frame structure of the novel; and Gayatri Spivak uses post-colonial criticism to suggest how *Frankenstein* undoes the oppositions upon which Western society is based.

The trend towards placing *Frankenstein* within a broader cultural context is also reflected in Tim Marshall's 1995 *Murdering to Dissect: Grave-Robbing, Frankenstein and the Anatomy Literature*, and in the 1994 collection of essays, *Frankenstein, Creation, and Monstrosity*, edited by Stephen Bann. *Frankenstein's* relationship with other literary texts is one focus of discussion in this collection. Robert Olorenshaw, for example, considers the treatment of the monster in Shelley's *Frankenstein* and Stoker's *Dracula*; Michael Fried examines monstrosity in *Frankenstein* and Wells's *The Island of Dr Moreau*; and Jasia Reichardt looks at *Frankenstein* in light of the wider treatment of monstrosity in science fiction. Other essays of particular interest in the collection include Michael Grant's examination of the adaptation of text into horror film in 'James Whale's *Frankenstein*: The Horror Film and the Symbolic Biology of the Cinematic Monster', and Crosbie Smith's discussion of Shelley's treatment of magic and natural sciences.

Frankenstein also attracts particular attention today because of the increasing concerns raised by scientific research in biomedicine, including cloning and xenografting. Susan Lederer has a useful chapter on this issue in her *Frankenstein: Penetrating the Secrets of Nature*, a book written to accompany a travelling exhibit of the same name. Other critics have considered the text in terms of modern techno-writing. Andrea Austin's 'Frankie and Johnny: Shelley, Gibson, and Hollywood's Love Affair with the Cyborg', for example, in the online journal, *Romanticism on the Net* , Vol. 21. 2001, explores the relationship between what she calls Mary Shelley's foundational cyborg story, *Frankenstein*, and William Gibson's 'Johnny Mnemonic', which is not only a re-working of the

CHECK THE BOOK

For a discussion of film versions of the novel, see Steven Earl Forry, *Hideous Progenies: Dramatizations of 'Frankenstein' from Mary Shelley to the Present*, 1990.

Frankenstein story, but also a foundational text of cyberpunk fiction. The primary trend in Shelley criticism today, however, seems to involve a movement away from *Frankenstein* to an exploration of her other works.

For those readers wishing to extend their study of Shelley beyond *Frankenstein*, Anne Mellor, in the excellent *Mary Shelley: Her Life, Her Fiction, Her Monsters*, has placed *Frankenstein* within the wider context of Shelley's other writings. Mellor, along with Audrey Fisch and Esther Schor, has also edited another collection of essays, *The Other Mary Shelley: Beyond Frankenstein*, which offers further analysis of Shelley's works. Kate Ellis considers Shelley's treatment of feminism, domesticity and radicalism in her later fiction, and relates this to the work of her mother, Mary Wollstonecraft. Other topics covered by these essays include Shelley's appropriation of classical myths, her use of the conventions of the travel literature of the time and her links with Romanticism.

CHECK THE BOOK

The bicentenary of Mary Shelley's birth in 1997 generated a number of publications in her honour. Two collections of essays are of particular note, which range over the entire canon of Shelley's work. *Mary Shelley in Her Times*, edited by Betty Bennett and Stuart Curran, 2000; and *Mary Shelley's Fictions*, edited by Michael Eberle-Sinatra, 2000.

PART FIVE

BACKGROUND

MARY SHELLEY

CHECK THE BOOK

For a scholarly but also eminently readable account of Shelley's life and world, which draws extensively upon journals and correspondence, see Miranda Seymour's *Mary Shelley*, 2000.

Mary Shelley was born in London on 30 August 1797, the only child of two notable intellectual radicals. Her father was the philosopher William Godwin (1756–1836), author of *Enquiry Concerning Political Justice*, 1793, which condemned all human institutions as corrupt and championed reason as the guide which would lead mankind to an ideal state. These ideas were presented in a fictional form in his *Caleb Williams*, 1794. Her mother was the pioneering feminist Mary Wollstonecraft (1759–97), author of *A Vindication of the Rights of Woman* , 1792, who died only ten days after her daughter's birth. Four years later, Godwin married the widowed Mary Jane Clairmont.

The relationship between daughter and stepmother was apparently strained. Mary nevertheless had an intellectually stimulating upbringing, associating with such friends of her father as Charles Lamb and Samuel Taylor Coleridge. In the spring of 1814, Mary began a relationship with Percy Bysshe Shelley, who was a frequent visitor to the Godwin's home. In the summer of 1814, Mary and Percy eloped. Accompanied by Mary's stepsister Jane (later known as 'Claire') Clairmont, they travelled through Europe before returning to England in the autumn. In London, they had a difficult first year. Percy Shelley was hounded by creditors, while Mary was alienated from her father, who refused to speak to her, and generally socially isolated. In 1815 she gave birth prematurely to a daughter who died soon afterwards.

CHECK THE BOOK

There are hundreds of entries on Mary Shelley's life, career, and writings in Lucy Morrison and Staci L. Stone, *A Mary Shelley Encyclopedia*, 2003.

The Shelleys' financial situation improved and they moved to Windsor in August of the same year. In January 1816 she gave birth to a son, William. Claire, meanwhile, had seduced George Gordon, Lord Byron (1788–1824), and was pregnant with his child. Mary, Shelley, and Claire joined Byron with his friend and personal physician John Polidori at the Villa Diodati by Lake Geneva. It was here that the events recounted in Mary's 1831 'Introduction' took place. Fanny Imlay, another of Mary's half-sisters, committed suicide in October 1816 and two months later Harriet Shelley drowned herself in the Serpentine, Hyde Park.

Mary and Percy immediately married and Godwin was soon reconciled with his daughter. Mary gave birth to a daughter, Clara, in September 1817, soon after the completion of *Frankenstein*. The novel was published anonymously in 1818 and the Shelleys left for Italy. Both of their children died soon after; another, Percy Florence Shelley, the only child of the marriage to survive into adulthood, was born in 1819. In August 1822, Percy Bysshe Shelley drowned in the Gulf of Spezia. Mary returned to England the following year and never remarried. She died in London on 1 February 1851 at the age of fifty-three.

HER OTHER WORKS

Although now known primarily as the author of *Frankenstein*, Mary Shelley was a prolific writer. She produced essays and reviews, travel books, mythological dramas and numerous biographies. She also edited her husband's *Poetical Works*, 1839, and his *Essays, Letters from Abroad, Translations and Fragments*, 1839, both generally considered marred by distortions and omissions which resulted in an overidealised portrait of the poet and his work. Shelley's last publication was *Rambles in Germany and Italy*, 1844, an account of her continental travels with her son, Percy Florence.

Shelley also wrote many short stories and was a frequent contributor to the 'Keepsake' Annuals of the time. While many of these stories are somewhat sentimental, in accordance with the kind of publication in which they were placed, others quite successfully pursue issues developed in the earlier *Frankenstein*. 'Transformation', 1831, for example, concerns another monster, this time a deformed Satanic dwarf; 'The Mortal Immortal', 1834, is the story of an alchemist's apprentice which examines the meaning and consequences of immortality; and 'The Mourner', 1830, again considers aggression, monstrosity, the **double** and family relationships.

CHECK THE BOOK

On Shelley's short stories see Sonia Hofkosh's 'Disfiguring Economies: Mary Shelley's Short Stories', in *The Other Mary Shelley: Beyond Frankenstein*, eds. Audrey Fisch, Anne Mellor, and Esther Schor, 1993.

 CHECK THE NET

An etext of *The Last Man* can be found at **http://www.rc.umd.edu/editions/mws/lastman/index.html**.

CHECK THE BOOK

If you would like to read some of Shelley's other works, you might be interested in Betty T. Bennett and Charles E. Robinson, eds., *The Mary Shelley Reader*, 1990.

Shelley's interest in the family and the domestic affections produces the main link between *Frankenstein* and her other novels. *Valperga*, 1823, and *The Last Man*, 1826, both locate the source of cultural disaster in man's renouncement of the world of domestic affections. *Valperga*, a historical romance set in fourteenth-century Italy, examines the destructive effects of ambition and egotism. *The Last Man*, a fantasy of cultural annihilation in the twenty-first century and usually considered Shelley's most significant work after *Frankenstein*, provides a pessimistic account of the evils of social institutions. This fantasy about the gradual destruction of the world by a plague is narrated by Verney, the last man on earth and, like the creature, a reworking of Adam. The novel draws heavily on one of the texts with which the creature becomes familiar: Volney's *Ruins of Empire[s]*.

Shelley's next novel, *Perkin Warbeck*, 1830, examines the manner in which political forces influence and control the individual and, as in *Frankenstein*, the way in which the domestic ideal is sacrificed to the desire for power. The primary family relationship for Shelley is that of father and daughter; mothers rarely survive long in her novels. Her most notorious examination of this relationship is in the novella *Mathilda*, an account of a father's incestuous desire for his daughter. Although completed in 1819, *Mathilda* was not published during Shelley's lifetime. *Lodore*, 1835, and *Falkner*, 1837, are, like *Mathilda*, set in early nineteenth-century English society and concerned primarily with the father-daughter relationship. It is in these later novels that Shelley is sometimes considered to provide her most conservative and sentimental celebration of the domestic affections, demonstrating the need for both men and women to set aside individual needs and desires in the interests of the well-being of the family. Even in these last novels, however, the **ambivalence** demonstrated in *Frankenstein* remains, and Mary Shelley tempers her celebration of the family with a recognition of the problems for women who define themselves purely in terms of their family roles and responsibilities.

LITERARY BACKGROUND

THE GOTHIC TRADITION

In her 1831 Introduction, Shelley declares her desire to 'curdle the blood, and quicken the beatings of the heart' (p. 8). This is the first of many signals to the reader that *Frankenstein* should be placed in the **genre** of the **Gothic**. Difficulties begin to arise, however, when we attempt to relate *Frankenstein* to other Gothic novels, as the term Gothic covers a wide variety of texts and is by no means simple to define. The 'classic' Gothic published during the period 1765–1820 most notably includes Horace Walpole's *The Castle of Otranto*, 1765, Ann Radcliffe's *The Mysteries of Udolpho*, 1794 and Matthew Lewis's *The Monk*, 1796. These texts are linked by what are traditionally considered conventional Gothic traits: the emphasis on fear and terror, the presence of the supernatural, the placement of events within a distant time and an unfamiliar and mysterious setting, and the use of highly stereotyped characters. If we were to limit our definition to these characteristics, however, it would be difficult to locate *Frankenstein* firmly within the Gothic genre. In spite of Shelley's claim to be writing a 'ghost story' there is nothing supernatural here; it is an emphatically secular and material world that she constructs. There are no decaying monasteries, no decadent monks, headless nuns, or terrifying brigands; castles are mentioned as though features of a travelogue rather than serving as the setting for supernatural events. All the conventional Gothic trappings have disappeared.

It is perhaps not surprising that Shelley should be wary of the traditional Gothic form. In 1818, when *Frankenstein* first appeared, the publication of Jane Austen's *Northanger Abbey* and Thomas Love Peacock's *Nightmare Abbey*, with their **parodic** use of Gothic **conventions**, suggested that the genre, once so popular it dominated the novel market, was losing credibility. Austen, in particular, pointed to the direction Gothic would now take when she demonstrated, with her criticism of her heroine's over-stimulated imagination, that real terror was produced in and by the mind, the human psyche, not by haunted castles and apparitions wandering through the night.

CHECK THE BOOK

For an introduction to the Gothic with entries on background and contexts, key writers and works, and common themes and topics, see Glennis Byron and David Punter, eds., *Gothic*, 2003.

QUESTION

How does Mary Shelley appropriate and revise Gothic motifs and conventions in *Frankenstein*?

When we turn towards recent definitions of the Gothic that are more concerned to tease out the Gothic essence than to list the surface trappings, we find an emphasis on this dark side of the human psyche. The Gothic is now considered an attempt to expose and explore the unconscious world of desires and fears that both society and the individual, in an attempt to maintain stability, attempt to suppress. Gothic writers are interested in the breakdown of boundaries, in the exploration of what is forbidden, in desires that should neither be spoken of or acted upon. They are concerned, above all, with excess and transgression. Reading *Frankenstein* as a Gothic novel, we might suggest that what Victor does and what Victor creates are unnatural. He goes too far, breaks the laws of nature, crosses forbidden boundaries, and what he unleashes, within himself and in society, is disruption and destruction. With suggestions of incest in Victor's love for his 'more than sister' (p. 36) Elizabeth, with the focus on a creative act that usurps the natural functions of both God and women and a creation that blurs the boundaries between life and death, with the allowance for the possibility that the creature is Victor's **doppelgänger**, acting out his forbidden desires, an expression of the darker side of his psyche, *Frankenstein* quite clearly fits within modern conceptions of the Gothic.

In its exploration of these concepts, its focus on the dark side of the psyche, *Frankenstein* also begins to emerge as a precursor of such later Victorian Gothic novels as Stevenson's *Dr Jekyll and Mr Hyde*, Wells's *The Island of Dr Moreau* and Wilde's *The Picture of Dorian Gray*. Like *Frankenstein*, these novels refuse to distance the reader from the horrors described but insist instead on the modernity of the setting and the concerns; they draw on science, not superstition, on what is frighteningly possible and familiar rather than entirely absurd and alien. They make an inescapable link between the world of the text and the world of the reader. They emphasise that the horror is in us, now.

THE ROMANTIC MOVEMENT

Frankenstein may be primarily a Gothic novel, but, as the many quotations from such poets as Coleridge suggest, the novel also has significant connections with the Romantic movement. The link

CHECK THE BOOK

E. J. Clery discusses Shelley's work in the context of female Gothic in *Women's Gothic: From Clara Reeve to Mary Shelley*, 2000.

CHECK THE FILM

Ken Russell's usually reviled film *Gothic*, 1986, is loosely based on the events at the Villa Diodati in the summer of 1816 that led to the writing of *Frankenstein*.

seems almost inevitable, given Mary's family background. Her father, Godwin, had a notable impact on many of the English Romantic poets and is mentioned frequently in their writings. Her husband, Percy Bysshe Shelley, was one of the key Romantic poets, and Mary was frequently in the company of such other notable Romantics as Lord Byron. While the influence of Romanticism on Mary Shelley is undeniable, it is nevertheless not quite so easy to decide what stand she is taking on the Romantic concerns that pervade *Frankenstein*. While in the past critics have gone so far as to call *Frankenstein* a handbook of Romanticism, they now frequently tend to see the novel more as a critique than a celebration of Romantic ideals.

Romanticism is as difficult to define as the Gothic; indeed, we now generally speak of Romanticisms to suggest the complexity of the phenomenon. Nevertheless, there are at least three defining characteristics which can be identified with some confidence as features of Romanticism that are also of specific relevance to Shelley's *Frankenstein*. There is a concern with radical social reform, a preoccupation with the role of the poet and the workings of the imagination, and an interest in nature.

The Romantic movement is usually considered to originate around 1789, the year of the French Revolution, optimistically seen by Godwin, Wordsworth, and others as the beginnings of a new age of justice and equality for all. Romanticism is politically inspired by both the French and American revolutions and by wars of independence throughout Europe. It was a time of social unrest and political activism, even in England. Many of the Romantics were initially full of the same optimism and idealism that inspired Godwin, who placed the source of evil in human institutions, insisted upon the importance of justice and equality for all, and believed in the perfectibility of the human race. Unlike Godwin, however, most found their idealism eventually conflicted with their experience and became disillusioned about the possibilities of reform through political action. Shelley's *Frankenstein* is certainly concerned with the corruption of social institutions, but she shows little faith in the possibility of change, and the creation of the creature, a new, improved man, suggests she has equally little faith in the perfectibility of the human race.

 CHECK THE NET

One of the main on-line sources of information about the Romantics and their works is at the Voice of the Shuttle: **http://vos.ucsb. edu/browse. asp?id=2750**.

CHECK THE BOOK

For a useful introduction to the Romantic movement, see Marilyn Butler, *Romantics, Rebels and Reactionaries. English Literature and Its Background*, 1981.

CHECK THE NET

Romantic Circles is a website devoted to the study of Romantic period literature and culture: **http://www.rc.umd.edu/**.

CHECK THE NET

Read excerpts from Edmund Burke's essay on the sublime at **http://www.publicbookshelf.com/public_html/** and explore the Outline of Great Books Volume I link.

In their championing of social progressive causes and their rejection of conventional social morals, many Romantics felt isolated, alienated from society as a whole. When they tried to transform the world through poetry, they were equally isolated. For the Romantics, the imagination is used both to escape the world and to transform it and such creativity is seen as powerful, God-like, leading to an emphasis on the assertion of the self and the value of individual experience. They become Promethean figures who rival and defy God himself, creating the world anew through poetry (see **Analogy and allusion**).

As the Romantics looked within to their own inner natures, they also looked without to the natural world around them. Reacting against the earlier eighteenth-century admiration for the ordered and cultivated, they became more interested in the wild and untamed aspects of nature. In this respect they were greatly influenced by Edmund Burke (1729–97) and his *Philosophical Enquiry into the Origin of Our Ideas of the Sublime and the Beautiful*, 1757. Burke defined the beautiful as that characterised by smallness, orderliness, smoothness, brightness; the **sublime**, however, was of much more interest to the Romantics, with its associations of darkness, solitude, infinity, of terror inspired by the gigantic and incomprehensible. While Shelley provides many sublime landscapes, it is difficult to decide whether or not she is celebrating them in the Romantic manner; her characters may, but does she? Is there inspiration in the icy mountainous landscape where Victor confronts the creature, in the Arctic regions where both meet their deaths, or do these sublime landscapes simply seem dangerous, alien, sterile? Do they stimulate and inspire or do they simply suggest alienation and the death of feeling? Perhaps these alien and barren landscapes have no more to do with humanity than Victor's egotistical Promethean desires.

While *Frankenstein* is generally identified as a Gothic novel with important links to the Romantic movement, critics have suggested that it has connections with many other genres. *Frankenstein* may be seen as the first work of science fiction, drawing as it does on scientific and technological advances and suggesting the possible future consequences of such developments (see **Historical**

background). Some critics have identified features which link it to the **sentimental novel**; some have placed it in the tradition of the **confessional novel** which included such other works as Godwin's *Caleb Williams*; others have suggested that the language and psychological interests of the novel identify it as a precursor of **realist** modes of writing. As the many conflicting critical views suggest, while *Frankenstein* may be associated with a wide variety of genres, the novel repeatedly refuses to be limited to any particular one. *Frankenstein* appears to be, as Muriel Spark suggests in *Child of Light*, a 'new and hybrid fictional species' (p. 128), and so it is quite appropriate that Mary Shelley should bring her 'Introduction' to a close with the words 'And now, once again, I bid my hideous progeny go forth and prosper' (p. 10). Both book and monster are constructed out of an assortment of sometimes ill-fitting bits and pieces, and perhaps, ultimately, we should consider whether *Frankenstein* may be more concerned with questioning the validity and restraints of classifications than with fitting comfortably into one specific form.

CHECK THE BOOK

Debra Benita Shaw begins *Women, Science, and Fiction: The Frankenstein Inheritance*, 2000, with a consideration of the role played by *Frankenstein* in the field of science fiction.

HISTORICAL BACKGROUND

Frankenstein was written at a time of great changes in British society and deals with a variety of issues central to the development of industrial Britain in the late eighteenth and early nineteenth centuries. This was a period of significant developments in science and technology and, at least partly as a result of such advances, also a time of social and political upheaval.

SOCIAL UNREST

Technological developments had a notable impact on people's lives, endangering traditional ways of living in much the same way as scientific developments undermined traditional beliefs. In the first stages of the Industrial Revolution the introduction of new technologies posed a significant threat to the livelihoods of many of the working class, frequently prompting violent reactions. The Luddite disturbances of 1811–17, during which factories and mills were attacked and machines destroyed, stirred uneasy memories of the bloodier excesses of the French Revolution of 1789. The French

CONTEXT

Percy Shelley's 'England in 1819', which remained unpublished until 1839, suggests concerns about the political system of the time which were shared by many. See an etext of this poem at **http://eir. library. utoronto.ca/rpo/ display/ poem1885.html**.

Revolution was initially seen by Godwin, Mary Shelley's father, and by Wordsworth as the sign of the start of a new era in history. The revolutionaries removed corrupt institutions and, like Godwin, believed in the perfectability of man. They could be said to be attempting to create a new man; but although their motives were admirable, the means they adopted were violent, and their execution of the King, traditionally considered the representative of the divine on earth, suggested defiance of God's laws. Some critics have suggested Shelley's monster may be read as an emblem of the French Revolution itself, a 'gigantic body politic', as Anne Mellor states, 'originating in a desire to benefit all mankind' but so abandoned and abused 'that it is driven into an uncontrollable rage' (p. 82).

CHECK THE NET

A comprehensive summary of the French Revolution can be found at **http://members. aol.com/ agentmess/ frenchrev/ summary.html**.

The Pentridge uprising of 1817, when 300 men marched towards Nottingham, expecting numerous other such marches throughout the country, was designed to overthrow the government and seemed to confirm the alarming possibility of working-class revolt in Britain. The possibility of such revolt always seems to simmer just below the surface of *Frankenstein*. When the leaders of the Pentridge uprising were executed in November, Percy Shelley responded with a political pamphlet deploring the state of a country torn between the alternatives of anarchy and oppression. Mary Shelley had radical sympathies, and through her depiction of the monster, she reveals an outraged awareness of social injustice and a passionate desire for reform. At the same time, she could not fully support rebellion against the established order, and, again through the monster, expresses fear of the revolutionary violence that injustice in society might provoke. Like Percy Shelley, she sees only the alternatives of anarchy and oppression.

SCIENTIFIC DEVELOPMENTS

Shelley's account of a scientist who creates a monster and refuses to take responsibility for the results of his experiments emerges at least partly out of her familiarity with and understanding of the scientific debates and discoveries of her time. During the later eighteenth century, traditional metaphysical and theological investigations into the meaning of life began to be displaced by secular and materialist explorations of its origins and nature. In 1771, Joseph Priestly observed that mice placed in a bell jar depleted the air and led to suffocation, while sprigs of mint refreshed the air and made the mice lively, and eight years later, Antoine Lavoisier interpreted Priestley's data to provide the first understanding of the processes of respiration. Many scientists, however, remained reluctant to accept a theory that made human life dependent upon the vegetative world; the idea that life might be either maintained or initiated simply through material causes challenged all traditional beliefs about humanity's unique position within the world.

By 1814, a debate over what came to be known as the 'life-principle' had caused a rift in the sciences, encapsulated primarily in the differing positions of John Abernethy, President of the Royal College of Surgeons, and his pupil William Lawrence, appointed as second Professor at the College in 1815. Lawrence advocated a strictly materialist position. Abernethy, wanting to retain some metaphysical elements in common with religious beliefs, conversely argued that such concepts as 'organisation', function' and 'matter' could not entirely explain life: something else was required, some 'subtle, active vital principle' that might be linked to the concept of the immortal soul.

In *Mary Shelley*, Anne Mellor convincingly demonstrates how closely Shelley relied upon the works of Humphrey Davy, Erasmus Darwin, and Luigi Galvani. Davy's pamphlet, *A Discourse, Introductory to a Course of Lectures on Chemistry*, 1802, provides Shelley with information about chemistry, with the suggestion that chemistry might provide the secret of life, and with material for Waldman's lectures. Shelley, like Davy, distinguishes the master-scientist who seeks to interfere with and control nature, to modify and change nature's creations, from the scholar-scientist who seeks only to understand. Unlike Davy, however, Shelley believed the former to be dangerous, the latter to be the good scientist, the type of scientist exemplified by Erasmus Darwin. While Percy Shelley, in his 1818 Preface, refers to Darwin as one of the scientists who have considered such an act of creation as 'not of impossible occurrence' (p. 13), Darwin, like his better-known grandson, Charles, was an evolutionist, not a creationist, and therefore directly opposed to the fictional Victor Frankenstein who wants to create and change life

CHECK THE NET

See a virtual exhibit on *Frankenstein: Mary Shelley's Dream* for information about the science and scientific instruments of the time: **http://www. thebakken.org/ Frankenstein/ exhibit.htm**.

CHECK THE BOOK

through chemical means and is not willing to wait for the slow processes of evolution. From this perspective Victor is, like Davy, the bad scientist, the one who interferes with and changes nature. Darwin is the good scientist who only observes and records.

It is specifically galvanism, however, to which Mary Shelley refers in *Frankenstein*. In 1791, Luigi Galvani published *Commentary on the Effects of Electricity on Muscular Motion* which suggested that animal tissue contained a vital force, which he dubbed 'animal electricity' but later came to be known as 'galvanism'. Galvani believed this was a different form of electricity from that produced by such things as lightning, that it was produced by the brain, conducted by the nerves, and produced muscular motion. This theory led to a variety of experiments on human corpses, the most notorious of which was carried out by Giovanni Adini on the corpse of the murderer Thomas Forster after he was hanged at Newgate. Wires were attached to stimulate galvanic activity and the corpse began to move, giving the appearance of re-animation. Such experiments as this were widely discussed in delightful detail in the popular press, and, as Mellor suggests, no doubt formed 'the scientific prototype of Victor Frankenstein, restoring life to dead bodies' (p. 125). Drawing upon scientific research, then, Shelley provides a frighteningly believable prediction of what the future might hold in a world where it is man, and no longer God, who holds the secret of life.

World events

1746 Invention of Leyden jar (prototype electrical condenser)

1752 Benjamin Franklin invents lightning conductor

1783 American independence recognised

1784 Benjamin Franklin, Antoine Lavoisier and others investigate Franz-Anton Mesmer's claims of a 'magnetic fluid' in man

1789 French Revolution begins

1790 Luigi Galvani 'discovers' electricity in animal and human limbs

Mary Shelley's life

1756 Father, William Godwin, born

1759 Mother, Mary Wollstonecraft, born

1792 Mother goes to Paris with Gilbert Imlay

Literary events

1667 Milton, *Paradise Lost*

1750 Jean-Jacques Rousseau expounds idea of 'noble savage'

1762 J.-J. Rousseau's *Emile* suggests child ideally be allowed full scope for development away from harmful influences of civilisation

1772 Goethe, *The Sorrows of Young Werther*

1787 Mary Wollstonecraft, *Thoughts on the Education of Daughters*

1791 Volney, *Ruins of Empire[s]* published

1792 Mary Wollstonecraft, *Vindication of the Rights of Women*

World events	Mary Shelley's life	Literary events
1793 Louis XVI beheaded		**1793** William Godwin, *An Enquiry Concerning Political Justice*
1794 Erasmus Darwin's *Zoonomia* discusses spontaneous generation	**1794** Mother has illegitimate daughter, Fanny	**1794** William Godwin, *Caleb Williams*. Thomas Paine's *The Age of Reason*. William Blake, *The Book of Urizen*
		1795 Sade, *Philosophie dans le Boudoir*
		1796 Mary Wollstonecraft, *Letters written during a Short Residence in Sweden, Norway and Denmark*
	1797 Mother and father marry. **Mary born**. Mother dies ten days later	
		1798 Coleridge, *The Rime of the Ancient Mariner*
1800 Alessandro Volta creates prototype electric battery		**1800** Maria Edgeworth, *Castle Rackrent*
	1801 Father remarries	
1803 Britain at war with France		
1804 Napoleon becomes emperor		
1805 Battle of Trafalgar		
1806 William Pitt dies		
1807 Slave Trade abolished in the British Empire		
		1808 Goethe, *Faust* (Part 1)
1811 Luddite riots		**1811** Jane Austen, *Sense and Sensibility*. Shelley, *The Necessity of Atheism*
1812 Napoleon retreats from Moscow		
		1813 Jane Austen, *Pride and Prejudice*

World events	Mary Shelley's life	Literary events
	1814 Mary begins affair with Shelley. Elopes to Continent. Shelley's *Refutation of Deism*	
	1815 Mary gives birth prematurely to daughter, who dies a few days later	
1816 First wooden stethoscope	**1816** Mary gives birth to son William. Mary and Shelley leave for Geneva. Shelley's wife Harriet drowns. Mary and Shelley marry	**1816** Jane Austen, *Emma*
	1817 Mary writing *Frankenstein*. Gives birth to daughter Clara	**1817** Lord Byron's *Manfred*
1818 First (unsuccessful) blood transfusions at Guy's Hospital, London	**1818** *Frankenstein* published. Family leave for Italy. Shelley writes *Prometheus Unbound* (publ. 1820). Daughter Clara dies in Venice	**1818** Thomas Love Peacock, *Nightmare Abbey*. Walter Scott, *Tales of my Landlord*
	1819 Son William dies. Mary writes *Mathilda*, a semi-autobiographical tale of incest. Son Percy born	
1820 George III dies		
1821 Napoleon dies	**1821** Mary writes *Valpurga*	
	1822 Shelley drowns at sea	
1824 Lord Byron dies	**1824** Mary begins work on *The Last Man*	
1827 Beethoven dies		
	1830 Mary publishes *Perkin Warbeck*	
	1831 Revised edition of Frankenstein	
		1832 Goethe, *Faust* (Part 2)
	1835 Mary publishes *Lodore*	
	1836 Mary's father dies	
	1837 Mary's *Falkner* published	
	1851 Mary Shelley dies	

Stephen Bann, *Frankenstein, Creation, and Monstrosity*, Reaktion, 1994
Places Frankenstein within broader, cultural context

Chris Baldick, *In Frankenstein's Shadow: Myth, Monstrosity and Nineteenth-century Writing*, Oxford University Press, 1990
The monster as mythic image in nineteenth-century literature

—— 'The Politics of Monstrosity,' in Botting, ed., *Frankenstein*, pp. 48–67
Interesting examination of the notion of monstrosity

Betty T. Bennett, ed., *The Letters of Mary Wollstonecroft Shelley*, 3 vols, Johns Hopkins University Press, 1988
Worthwhile background reading

—— and Stuart Curran, eds, *Mary Shelley in her Times*, Johns Hopkins University Press, 2000
Useful collection of essays

—— and Charles Robinson, eds, *The Mary Shelley Reader*, Oxford University Press, 1990
Includes some of Shelley's other works

Fred Botting, *Gothic*, Routledge, 1996
Best introduction to the Gothic

—— *Making Monstrous: Frankenstein, Criticism, Theory*, Manchester University Press, 1991
Challenging poststructuralist analysis for the advanced reader

—— ed., *Frankenstein*, Macmillan, 1995
An extremely useful collection of the most significant essays written on *Frankenstein*; the novel is examined from a wide variety of critical perspectives

Peter Brooks, '"Godlike Science/Unhallowed Arts": Language, Nature, and Monstrosity,' in Levine and Knoepflmacher, eds, pp. 205–20

Marilyn Butler, *Romantic Rebels and Reactionaries: English Literature and its Background*, Oxford University Press, 1981
Very useful introduction to the Romantic movement

Glennis Byron and David Punter, eds, *Gothic*, Blackwell, 2003
Includes material on background, context, key writings, common themes and topics

E.J. Clery, *Women's Gothic: From Clara Reeve to Mary Shelley*, Northcote Press, 2000
Discusses Shelley's work in the context of female Gothic

Jeffrey Jerome Cohen, *Monster Theory. Reading Culture*, University of Minnesota Press, 1991
General exploration of representation and conceptions of monstrosity through the ages

Aidan Day, *Romanticism*, Routledge, 1996
  Useful introduction to the ideas of Romanticism

Michael Eberle-Sinatra, ed., *Mary Shelley's Fiction*, Palgrave, 2000
  Useful collection of essays

—— 'Science, Gender and Otherness in Shelley's *Frankenstein* and Kenneth Branagh's Film Adaptation', *European Romantic Review*, 9..2.1988
  Discusses the effects of Branagh's changes to the original novel

Kate Ellis, 'Monsters in the Garden: Mary Shelley and the Bourgeois Family,' in Levine, pp. 123–142
  Reads Victor's rebellion as a rebellion against the family

—— 'Subversive Surfaces: The Limits of Domestic Affection in Mary Shelley's Later Fiction,' in Fisch *et al.*, pp. 220–34
  Literary historical approach

Paula Feldman and Diana Scott-Kilvert, eds, *The Journals of Mary Shelley, 1814–1844*, 2 vols, Clarendon Press, 1987
  Well worth reading

Audrey A. Fisch, Anne Mellor, and Esther Schor, eds. *The Other Mary Shelley*: *Beyond Frankenstein* (Oxford University Press, 1993)
  Collection of essays on Shelley's other works

Steven Earl Forry, *Hideous Progenies: Dramatization of Frankenstein from Shelley to the Present*, University of Pennsylvania Press, 1990
  Discusses the different ways the relationship between Frankenstein and the Monster is handled in film

Michael Fried, 'Impressionist Monsters: H.G Wells's *The Island of Dr Moreau*,' in Bann, pp. 95–112
  Compares treatment of monsters in Wells and Shelley

Sandra M. Gilbert, and Susan Gubar, *The Madwoman in the Attic: The Woman Writer and the Nineteenth-Century Literary Imagination*, Yale University Press, 1979
  Feminist criticism

Michael Grant, 'James Whale's *Frankenstein*: The Horror Film and the Symbolic Biology of the Cinematic Monster,' in Bann, pp. 113–35
  Considers the adaptation of text into film

Kenneth Gross, 'Satan and the Romantic Satan', in Margaret Ferguson and Mary Nyquist, eds, *Re-Membering Milton: Essays on the Texts and Traditions,* Methuen, 1987
  Discusses Romantic attitude to Satan

R. Glynn Grylls, *Mary Shelley: A Biography*, Oxford University Press, 1938
  Superseded by Mellor

Judith Halberstam, *Skin Shows: Gothic Horror and the Technology of Monsters*, Duke University Press, 1995
  Places *Frankenstein* in the context of Gothic monstrosity

James Heffernan, 'Looking at the Monster, *Frankenstein* and Film', *Critical Inquiry*, 21.1.1997
  Looks at the many different ways the Monster has been treated in film

Sonia Hofkosh, 'Disfiguring Economies: Mary Shelley's Short Stories' in Fisch et al., eds, 1993

Margaret Homans, 'Bearing Demons: *Frankenstein's* Circumvention of the Material,' in Botting, pp. 140–165
  Uses Lacanian psychoanalysis and deconstruction

Gary Kelly, *English Fiction of the Romantic Period: 1789–1830*, Longman, 1989
  Provides useful background information and includes a brief discussion of *Frankenstein*

Robert Kiely, *The Romantic Novel in England*, Harvard University Press, 1972
  Generic study

Susan E. Lederer, *Frankenstein: Penetrating the Secrets of Nature*, Rutgers University Press, 2002
  Interesting new approach to *Frankenstein*

George Levine, and U.C. Knoepflmacher, eds, *The Endurance of Frankenstein: Essays on Mary Shelley's Novel*, University of California Press, 1979
  Useful collection of essays that changed the course of *Frankenstein* criticism. Good place to start further research

Tim Marshall, *Murdering to Dissect: Grave-Robbing, Frankenstein and the Anatomy Literature*, Manchester University Press, 1995
  Literary historical approach

Anne Mellor, *Mary Shelley: Her Life, Her Fiction, Her Monsters*, Routledge, 1988
  Excellent for both biographical information and a clear analysis of the whole range of Shelley's work

Ellen Moers, 'Female Gothic,' in Levine, pp. 77–87
  Reads *Frankenstein* as a birth myth

Tim Morton, *A Routledge Literary Sourcebook on Mary Shelley's Frankenstein*, Routledge, 2002
  Useful source on literary and cultural contexts

Beth Newman, 'Narratives of Seduction and the Seductions of Narrative: The Frame Structure of *Frankenstein*,' in Botting, pp. 166–90
  Deconstructive reading of frame structure

Paul O'Flynn, 'Production and Reproduction: The Case of *Frankenstein*,' in Botting, pp. 21–47
  Marxist reading focusing on how political and economic conditions shape the text

Robert Olorenshaw, 'Narrating the Monster: From Mary Shelley to Bram Stoker,' in Bann, pp. 158–76
  Comparison of the treatment of the monster in *Frankenstein* and *Dracula*

Mary Poovey, '"My Hideous Progeny": Mary Shelley and the Feminization of Romanticism,' *PMLA*, 95, 1980, pp. 332–47
  Feminist criticism

Jasia Reichardt, 'Artificial Life and the Myth of *Frankenstein*,' in Bann, pp. 135–57
  Considers monstrosity in the context of science fiction

Berthold Schoene-Harwood, ed., *Mary Shelley. Frankenstein: A Reader's Guide to Contemporary Criticism*, Palgrave, 2000
  A useful selection and discussion of the commentary on *Frankenstein*, from the first reviews in 1818 to postmodern readings of the mid-1990s

Esther Schor, ed., *The Cambridge Companion to Mary Shelley*, Cambridge University Press, 2003
  Collection of essays covering Shelley as biographer, editor, travel writer as well as author of fiction

Peter Dale Scott, 'Vital Artifice: Mary, Percy, and the Psychopolitical Integrity of *Frankenstein*,' in Levine, pp. 172–204

Miranda Seymour, *Mary Shelley*, John Murray, 2000
  A highly readable account of her life

Debra Benita Shaw, *Women, Science and Fiction: The Frankenstein Inheritance*, Palgrave, 2000
  Highlights significance of *Frankenstein* in the field of science fiction

Crosbie Smith, '*Frankenstein* and Natural Magic,' in Bann, pp. 39–59

Johanna Smith, *Mary Shelley: Frankenstein*, Palgrave, 2000
  The 1831 text presented with critical essays from contemporary psychoanalytic, Marxist, feminist and cultural studies perspectives

FURTHER READING

Muriel Spark, *Child of Light: A Reassessment of Mary Shelley*, Tower Bridge Publications, 1951
Critical biography

Gayatri Chakravorty Spivak, 'Three Women's Texts and a Critique of Imperialism,' in Botting, pp. 235–60
Post-colonial criticism shows how the text undoes the oppositions upon which Western individualism is based

Staci L. Stone, *A Mary Shelley Encyclopedia*, Greenwood Press, 2003
Much useful information on her life, career and writings

William Veeder, *Mary Shelley and Frankenstein: The Fate of Androgyny*, University of Chicago Press, 1986
Freudian/Lacanian analysis

J.R. Watson, *English Poetry of the Romantic Period: 1789–1830*, 2nd edn, Longman, 1992
Provides useful background information

allusion a reference, often only indirect, to another text, person, event, etc.

ambiguity when something can be interpreted in more than one way, often used to suggest uncertainty in meaning

ambivalence simultaneous existence of two different attitudes towards one idea, event, person, etc.

analogy illustration of an idea by means of a more familiar idea that is similar or parallel to it in some way

antagonist the most prominent character who opposes the protagonist

anti-hero central character who lacks the qualities expected in traditional heroes

antithesis a contrast or opposition

atmosphere rather vague term to suggest mood or emotional tone

closure ending, the process of ending

confessional novel appearing to deal with intimate experiences of narrator's life

connotation an association evoked by a word or phrase

conventions established practices or conspicuous features which occur repeatedly in particular kinds of works

dichotomy division into two parts or classifications

doppelgänger or **double** an alter-ego

epigraph quotation or phrase placed at start of a book

epistolary written in the form of a series of letters

epithet a word or phrase used to define a characteristic quality of a person

genre a kind; literary type or style

Gothic tradition see **Literary background**

imagery use of language to evoke sense-impressions

melodrama sensational drama, emotionally exaggerated

metaphor one thing is described in terms of its resemblance to another

narratee the imagined person within the text whom the narrator addresses

narrative perspective or **point of view** the way in which the narrator sees or interprets. **Embedded narrative** a story enclosed within a **frame narrative**, a tale within a tale. **Linear narrative** moves chronologically from beginning to end

narrator the person, as distinct from the author, who is telling the story. Narrators are variously categorised. **First-person narrators** present themselves as an 'I' who is involved in or witness to the events described. **Third-person narrators** are outside the story and refer to all characters as 'he' or 'she'. Within the third-person point of view can be distinguished the **omniscient narrator** who seems to know everything about the characters and events and has access to the minds of all, and the **limited narrator** who knows only what is thought and experienced by one character who is defined as the centre of consciousness

noble savage an idea developed by the French philosopher, Jean-Jacques Rousseau that man in primitive society is more noble than modern urban man, corrupted by civilisation

Oedipal conflict the repressed but continuing desire in the male adult to possess the mother and destroy the father. Freud drew the term from the tragedy of Oedipus

oxymoron combination of contradictory words

panegyric a public speech or poem of wholehearted praise

paradox an apparently contradictory statement which is nevertheless somehow meaningful

parallelism arrangement of similar words or presentation of characters to suggest correspondences between them

parody imitation of another work, often in order to make it amusing or ridiculous

protagonist leading character in a story

realism term most closely associated with a type of nineteenth-century novel which attempts to give the impression that it represents life and the world as a part of everyday reality, that such characters might exist, and such events actually occur

rhetoric the deliberate exploitation of eloquence for persuasive effect

sentimental novel emotionally extravagant novel, also called novel of sentiment, that became popular in late eighteenth century

simile one thing is likened to another through the use of 'like' or 'as'

sophism false but persuasive argument

sublime quality of awesome grandeur, as distinguished from the beautiful, in nature

symbol something representing something else, often an idea or quality, by analogy or association

tone rather vague term to suggest mood or atmosphere

voice rather vague term suggesting differences in tone and style

AUTHOR OF THESE NOTES

Glennis Byron is a Reader in English Studies at the University of Stirling. She is the editor of *Dracula*, Broadview, 1997 and *Nineteenth-Century Stories by Women*, Broadview, 1995, and the author of *Letitia Landon: The Woman Behind L.E.L.*, Manchester, 1995.

General editor

Martin Gray, former Head of the Department of English Studies at the University of Stirling, and of Literary Studies at the University of Luton

Maya Angelou
I Know Why the Caged Bird Sings

Jane Austen
Pride and Prejudice

Alan Ayckbourn
Absent Friends

Elizabeth Barrett Browning
Selected Poems

Robert Bolt
A Man for All Seasons

Harold Brighouse
Hobson's Choice

Charlotte Brontë
Jane Eyre

Emily Brontë
Wuthering Heights

Shelagh Delaney
A Taste of Honey

Charles Dickens
David Copperfield
Great Expectations
Hard Times
Oliver Twist

Roddy Doyle
Paddy Clarke Ha Ha Ha

George Eliot
Silas Marner
The Mill on the Floss

Anne Frank
The Diary of a Young Girl

William Golding
Lord of the Flies

Oliver Goldsmith
She Stoops to Conquer

Willis Hall
The Long and the Short and the Tall

Thomas Hardy
Far from the Madding Crowd
The Mayor of Casterbridge
Tess of the d'Urbervilles
The Withered Arm and other Wessex Tales

L.P. Hartley
The Go-Between

Seamus Heaney
Selected Poems

Susan Hill
I'm the King of the Castle

Barry Hines
A Kestrel for a Knave

Louise Lawrence
Children of the Dust

Harper Lee
To Kill a Mockingbird

Laurie Lee
Cider with Rosie

Arthur Miller
The Crucible
A View from the Bridge

Robert O'Brien
Z for Zachariah

Frank O'Connor
My Oedipus Complex and Other Stories

George Orwell
Animal Farm

J.B. Priestley
An Inspector Calls
When We Are Married

Willy Russell
Educating Rita
Our Day Out

J.D. Salinger
The Catcher in the Rye

William Shakespeare
Henry IV Part I
Henry V
Julius Caesar
Macbeth
The Merchant of Venice
A Midsummer Night's Dream
Much Ado About Nothing

Romeo and Juliet
The Tempest
Twelfth Night

George Bernard Shaw
Pygmalion

Mary Shelley
Frankenstein

R.C. Sherriff
Journey's End

Rukshana Smith
Salt on the snow

John Steinbeck
Of Mice and Men

Robert Louis Stevenson
Dr Jekyll and Mr Hyde

Jonathan Swift
Gulliver's Travels

Robert Swindells
Daz 4 Zoe

Mildred D. Taylor
Roll of Thunder, Hear My Cry

Mark Twain
Huckleberry Finn

James Watson
Talking in Whispers

Edith Wharton
Ethan Frome

William Wordsworth
Selected Poems

A Choice of Poets

Mystery Stories of the Nineteenth Century including The Signalman

Nineteenth Century Short Stories

Poetry of the First World War

Six Women Poets

For the AQA Anthology:

Duffy and Armitage & Pre-1914 Poetry

Heaney and Clarke & Pre-1914 Poetry

Poems from Different Cultures